HOWARD PHILLIPS LOVECRAFT:
DREAMER ON THE NIGHTSIDE

ALSO BY FRANK BELKNAP LONG

PAPER BOOKS

It was the Day of the Robot
Space Station 1
Survival World
The Three Faces of Time

EBOOKS

The Frank Belknap Long Science Fiction MEGAPACK®
The Second Frank Belknap Long Science Fiction MEGAPACK®
The Third Frank Belknap Long Science Fiction MEGAPACK®
The Frank Belknap Long Science Fiction Novel MEGAPACK®
The Frank Belknap Long Weird Fiction MEGAPACK®
The Second Frank Belknap Long Weird Fiction MEGAPACK®

HOWARD PHILLIPS LOVECRAFT: DREAMER ON THE NIGHTSIDE

FRANK BELKNAP LONG

WILDSIDE PRESS

TO LYDA
A gift from the far-off days
Of my still stubbornly recurrent youth
And—A gift from tomorrow

This book has been prepared and published with the kind permission and assistance of Lily Doty, Mansfield M. Doty, and the family of Frank Belknap Long.

Copyright © 1975 by Frank Belknap Long.

Published by Wildside Press LLC.
www.wildsidebooks.com

PREFACE

Aside from the associational ties inseparable from family relationships and childhood friendships, I have always felt that I knew Howard Phillips Lovecraft better than anyone else. From the early 1920s to the year of his death, I exchanged numerous letters with him, and met and talked with him at length at least 500 times—in New York, in Providence, and in the New England seacoast towns of great historical or antiquarian interest.

There are others, however, whose gifts of scholarship and capacity to devote long hours to patient research would make them better equipped to write a full-scale biography of HPL. Even if I were capable of undertaking such a task, I would be compelled to leave out many of the personal recollections set down in these pages. There is such an abundance of material which, objectively considered, no biographer would be justified in omitting, that he would have to impose upon himself a rigid standard of selectivity long before he reached the final chapter.

For several years now I have wanted to assemble a portrait of HPL which would be based largely upon my memories of him during those fifteen years of close and treasured friendship. I use the word "assemble" advisedly, being mindful of the fact that it is not always considered a wise approach in the realm of portraiture. It is not an easy task to take a series of random memories and fit them together in such a way that the portrait becomes all one piece with few, if any, irregularities. Whether I have succeeded or not, I shall leave to the judgment of the reader. I can think of no more important criterion, for success or failure must always be determined by a fairly large number of objective appraisals.

While not omitting all strictly biographical material, I have confined myself just to those periods of his childhood and early youth which he frequently discussed with me in detail, or those later periods which preceded the beginning of our correspondence but which seemed to me to possess some unusual relevance.

There must of necessity be omissions, even in a book of this nature. I could perhaps have shed a bit more of a revolving-prism light on some of HPL's meetings with his other friends of the period at which I was also present. But in many instances that light would have been minimal, for those meetings were often of brief duration and far less important, in a general way, than the longer Kalem Club gatherings at which all of his friends were present. Other aspects of those years which would bulk very large in a full-scale biography have been omitted for a different reason—they are fully and accurately preserved elsewhere, either in previous Arkham House volumes or in periodical articles about HPL, and thus no purpose would be served by including them.

Two of these accounts are typical of the others. W. Paul Cook of Athol, Massachusetts was also one of HPL's oldest friends and correspondents, and a companion on many occasions. But although Cook published my first volume of verse, *A Man from Genoa,* I exchanged no more than a few brief letters with him, and I met him only twice. HPL was not present at those encounters, and while he often mentioned Paul in his correspondence, the tribute he paid to him was invariably a simple one: "a gentleman of great scholarly attainments and one of the shining lights of amateur journalism." From meeting and talking with Cook I could have added merely that he was slightly stoutish and balding, and a brilliant conversationalist. In his own privately printed reminiscence, Cook provided an admirable portrayal of HPL—discerning, warmly sympathetic, and graced by no small measure of literary skill. But that memoir also is on record elsewhere, having been reprinted more than once.

The other instance I have characterized as typical of the omissions in general—and to discuss them all would run this preface to inordinate length!—concerns August Derleth's keen perception in encouraging Zealia Bishop to write an article about HPL for the 1953 Arkham House volume, *The Curse of Yig.* Mrs. Bishop was the most important of HPL's several revision clients, and his ghost-writing activities on her behalf are fully treated in that article. She discusses at length her first meeting with HPL and the most memorable of the stories which appeared under her name in *Weird Tales.* There is little I could have added to that account beyond calling attention to the fact that her memory appears to have failed her just once: I had nothing whatever to do with the writing of *The Mound*. That brooding, somber, and magnificently atmospheric story is Lovecraftian from the first page to the last. I could mention one thing more, however, which can hardly be considered of minor importance. Mrs. Bishop was a woman of great charm and quite exceptional beauty.

August Derleth's own biographical study of HPL contains much material of absorbing interest which I have not included in this volume because, as with the other instances cited, the reader has but to turn to it for several hours of the most rewarding enlightenment. This memoir is unique in that the number of dedicated Lovecraftians unfamiliar with it might be counted on one of those fringed and primitive adding devices that contain no more than ten or twelve beads.

I have made no deliberate effort to keep a few of these pages from verging on what a post-impressionistic painter might well have felt was the only proper way of depicting HPL, if only because no earlier school of painting could have done justice to his nightside genius. But in the main I have tried to keep in mind the more classic schools, and in no instance have I altered an actual occurrence, even in the smallest of particulars. However uncannily in accord with Jung's theory of synchronicity as two or three of these occurrences may seem, they actually happened. And I have resisted every impulse to parallel, on a verbal plane, the further extensions of pictorial art which gave birth to cubism, surrealism, and pre-World War I Germanic expressionism—except in three or four brief paragraphs!

—Frank Belknap Long

CHAPTER ONE

There possibly may be some readers of this volume who are unfamiliar with all but two or three of Lovecraft's most widely anthologized stories, or who know of him only through screen adaptations which thus far have tragically failed to do his writing justice. Other readers may be unacquainted with even the bare, skeletal outlines of his life apart from his writing, despite the far from scanty biographical material concerning him which has appeared in both Europe and America in the past few years. Such readers would feel justifiably cheated if I failed to devote at least one chapter to a generalized summary of the peak aspects of his growing fame.

There are some writers so closely linked to the legends which their lives have created that a kind of umbilical cord unites both aspects of their renown. Although cutting it would perhaps not diminish their actual literary stature, it is only when both aspects are considered as a totality that a figure of extraordinary fascination emerges. Howard Phillips Lovecraft, the dreamer and myth-maker of Providence, Rhode Island, was such a writer.

Interest in Lovecraft today is sweeping American college campuses on an unprecedented scale. At Brown University where thousands of his letters are on deposit in the John Hay Library, there are two groups of students numbering well over a hundred undergraduates, who conduct frequent excursions to sites which have figured prominently in his stories, and who hold ghost-watching vigils in awed expectation of seeing some spectral presence arise from a shadowed recess between two old houses with small-paned windows, or from the cypress-shadowed fringes of a Providence graveyard that was not unknown to Poe.

In well over fifty other colleges from coast to coast, similar circles have been formed. And in more than 200 colleges there are individual students whose interest in Lovecraftian lore absorbs them, when they are not attending classes, to the exclusion of almost everything else. There are Lovecraft groups at UCLA, Boston University, the University of Minnesota, and the University of the City of New York. At Georgia Southwestern College, "The Miskatonic Literary Circle" (after a place name invented by HPL) includes more than fifty members and provides an opportunity for both students and faculty interested in Lovecraft to meet and exchange ideas.

Several MA theses and one PhD thesis have thus far been written about Lovecraft, and more appear in immediate prospect. But interest in Lovecraft is far from confined to university campuses—he enjoys both a serious literary reputation and a popular readership that may be "cult figure" oriented to some extent, but which is entirely in accord with the fascinating, pluralistic kind of fame that seems to have a way of attaching itself to strikingly original writers, painters, and musicians.

To cite just two examples: in France during the mid-1840s, Gautier acquired much the same kind of fame by becoming the romantic forerunner of all bohemian artists, whether poets, novelists, or painters; and in Victorian England, Swinburne likewise possessed a "cult figure" popularity which in his youth seldom failed to keep pace with his serious literary renown as a major poet. It caused his followers of the period to go parading in long processions at Oxford, Cambridge, and even through the streets of London, reciting with wild abandonment many stanzas from *Poems and Ballads.*

HPL, of course, was a quite different kind of writer, and far less likely to win the allegiance of youthful extroverts. But among the young for whom the mystery and strangeness of cosmic realms can create a miraculous merging of reality and dream, his influence is becoming just as great.

In France today Lovecraft has become far more than just one of perhaps twenty widely read and discussed American writers of the twentieth century. He occupies an almost unique position in the realm in which Poe has remained unchallenged since the age of Baudelaire, and in France that realm has always been considered one of the most important branches of literature. To excel as a master of the macabre, as well as a cosmic myth-maker not unlike the Poe of *Eureka,* is to achieve a double kind of distinction, both in the eyes of the French intelligentsia and to others who would shun that label, preferring to think of themselves simply as lovers of imaginative literature who know when an original and powerful writer has crossed the Atlantic to cast a new and special kind of spell.

There is such an abundance of both early and quite recent critical tribute in France that not all the material could be included without imparting to this chapter the sort of bibliographical cast I have sought to avoid in the pages which follow, but some of it can be mentioned here without incurring such a risk. A few years before his death, Jean Cocteau hailed Lovecraft as the peer of Poe, but he was not the only prominent Gallic literary figure to have equated the best of Lovecraft with the best of Poe. He has received an even higher tribute from Jacques Bergier, who regards him as superior to Poe, both as a literary craftsman and as a spell-caster extraordinary in the realm of the marvelous. (Perhaps the soundness of Bergier's judgment may be open to dispute, because he has graciously called my *The Hounds of Tindalos* "one of the ten most terrifying and significant short stories in all literature." But everyone at times makes a few forgivable errors in judgment—eminently forgivable by me at least!—and one has to remember I would never have written that particular story had I not explored with HPL the dark, multidimensional corridors through which we both wound our way in pursuit of unnamable presences older than Time. If I had never met and talked with HPL, I am quite certain there would have been no *The Hounds of Tindalos* for Jacques Bergier to praise!)

Some five years ago Maurice Lévy, a young professor at the University of Toulouse, visited America on a Fulbright Scholarship to consult the Lovecraft letters at Brown University. I had the very great pleasure of meeting him at the time, and his recently published book about HPL bears a title which is indicative of how universal this author's fame has become in France. The title is simply *Lovecraft*—just that and nothing more. Had it not been for Professor Levy's New York visit, I would not have known at the time that classroom discussions of Lovecraft had taken place at the Sorbonne, as well as his own university, and that *L'Herne,* one of the two or three most important French literary journals, had declared HPL to be "the foremost American writer of supernatural literature in the past two centuries." Among the most notable of the books containing Lovecraft tributes have been Marcel Schneider's *La litterature fantantique en France* (1964), Tzvetan Todorov's *Introduction a la litterature fantastique* (1970), and *L'Amerique fantastique de Poe a Lovecraft* (1973). (The occurrence of "fantastique" in the titles of all three volumes is a tribute to Gallic perceptiveness, for there is no other adjective that conjures up so instantly, in an all-embracing way, the literature of the weird, the strange, and the marvelous.) This last handsome volume includes an excellent introduction by Jacques Finné.

In America an article by Edmund Wilson published in *The New Yorker* in 1945 discussed the incredible following which Lovecraft had acquired even at that early date. While not really a favorable review, the very fact that a critic of Wilson's renown felt the need to devote two or three full columns to *The Outsider* in so prestigious a publication suggests strongly that he was more uncertain on the matter of Lovecraft's nightside genius than he was willing to concede. If one reads between the lines of that review, the impression becomes inescapable that such was the case; when a critic is moved despite himself and without quite knowing the reason, his indignation can become a kind of self-protective weapon that can diminish the danger, real or fancied, of being assailed by some unknown dimension with which he would otherwise have been powerless to cope.

Articles about HPL are appearing everywhere today, both in the smaller journals and in publications of mass circulation, most notably in the *New York Times Book Review* and in the June 11, 1973 issue of *Time*. (Marc Slonim, "European Notebook," *New York Times Book Review,* 17 May 1970, pp. 10-14; Philip Herrera, "The Dream Lurker," *Time,* 11 June 1973, pp. 99-100.) There has even been a series of drawings in *Playboy,* by the gifted young artist Gahan Wilson, which are unmistakably based on Lovecraftian characters, although not identified as such.

Lovecraft's own fiction has in recent years appeared in many hardcover and paperback anthologies bearing the imprint of major publishers, and his stories have been translated into at least eighteen foreign languages. There have been seven screen productions based on the Cthulhu Mythos and on his earlier, more macabre tales, in addition to a number of radio and television adaptations. (I am not terribly happy with these film productions, for they fail to do justice to the cosmic sweep and realistic power of the Mythos and have been marred as well by the introduction of ridiculous, Hollywood-like intrusions on a "romantic interest" level, with one or two erotic incidents which would be perfectly legitimate in a different kind of dramatization, but which would have appalled Lovecraft—not for prudish reasons, but simply because such material has nothing to do with the Mythos.)

Most astonishing of all, perhaps, is the interest displayed in Lovecraft by various intellectual groups. HPL of course was the most fascinating of letter writers—his philosophical, aesthetic, and sociopolitical views are set forth on page after page in which no reading pause becomes possible. As an explorer of the unknown unique in our time, Lovecraft has aroused the admiration of many divergent philosophical circles which among themselves hold totally irreconcilable approaches to reality.

During his lifetime Lovecraft's knowledge of surrealism, for example, was of an exceedingly restricted nature. He was familiar with it only in the domain of painting, and although he had, of course, found many parallels between the work of the early Flemish artists and that of Dali and others, I am quite certain that even twentieth century surrealistic painting influenced him very little. He preferred Dunsanian dream landscapes in the realm of literature, and in actual artwork the macabre paintings and drawings of Goya, not because of their realism, but because they conjured up horrific visions.

Yet as early as 1943, there appeared in the American surrealist journal *VVV* the following tribute:

"Lovecraft recalls Dunsany, Algernon Blackwood, Arthur Machen and Poe. He frees himself from the conventions of fiction in its standardized forms, and presents an uncensored testimony of his inner adventures." (Robert Allerton Parker, "Such Pulp as Dreams Are Made On," *VVV,* Nos. 2-3 [March 1943], p. 64.)

It is an "uncensored testimony" of that nature which forms the foundation upon which present day surrealism has built much of its structural cohesiveness, and though many of its tenets would doubtlessly have been rejected by HPL, this aspect of surrealism is certainly in accord with what he most wanted to achieve.

The Chilean surrealistic painter Roberto Matta appears to have been directly influenced by Lovecraft and the Cthulhu Mythos, notably in such chilling masterpieces of the macabre as *Rghuin monstrous triumphs* and *Icrogy fecundated,* (Sarane Alexandrian, *Surrealistic Art* [New York: Praeger Publishers, Inc., 1970], p. 168.) while the American surrealist poet, artist, and critic, Franklin Rosemont (a long-time admirer of both Lovecraft and Clark Ashton Smith) has found similar Cthulhu Mythos motifs in the even more brilliant paintings of Jorge Camacho, including one of my "Hounds of Tindalos" coming in through angles.

HPL has also received many tributes from writers whose views are of an entirely non-surrealistic nature and who believe that only experimental laboratory science is capable of forging a key that can unlock the portals which guard the major mysteries. And this is as it should be. An author who totally lacks the capacity to set diametrically opposing schools into conflict can never be other than minor, for there are contradictions in every aspect of human experience with which the significant writer must struggle. Unless he has been whirled about by a few maelstroms of the inner mind, his guidance on a mountain-scaling expedition is unlikely to prove of much value, particularly in the realm of the unknown.

HPL was never a narrow, rigidly unyielding positivist, but he did have a great deal of respect for what is commonly thought of as "sound science" and refused to abandon what he believed might well be the truth about the universe: that it was wholly mechanistic, some vast, unknowable kind of rhythmic pulsation that had always existed and always would exist, and that this rhythm creates for us everything we perceive as reality—the whole of nature, animate and inanimate, on this planet and throughout the universe of stars.

I have always been willing to concede that such a possibility might well be the answer, but I have also been willing to believe that it might not. At times HPL himself questioned that possibility to some extent, although *my* questioning went just a bit further than he was willing to countenance without a protest. And he may well have been justified, who knows? I could be totally in error for believing that the universe may be even more mysterious than is remotely suggested by the cosmic rhythm hypothesis.

Just one concluding tribute to the variegated nature of HPL's appeal must be mentioned. A brilliant mathematician of my acquaintance, Donald R. Burleson, has recently dedicated to HPL a college textbook that is filled from cover to cover with—to me—rather awe-inspiring equations. This is undoubtedly the first time that a mathematical textbook has ever been dedicated to Lovecraft. But I doubt if it will be the last.

CHAPTER TWO

Much of the statistical material in the preceding chapter might have been somewhat abbreviated if all readers of this volume possessed the specialized knowledge of Lovecraftian lore that has become more widespread today than is commonly supposed, making him almost unique in that respect among literary figures of the past half-century. But, as I have previously stressed, a few readers might possibly have purchased this volume out of sheer fascination with his very name (which the author of the surrealistic article just quoted describes as "slightly incredible, but not a *nom de plume*"), while a larger number would feel grievously and quite justifiably resentful if I failed to include such basic biographical details as the date of his birth, his parentage, the dates of his arrival in New York and return to Providence, and a generalized summary of the stories as well. All this material will be elaborated upon later, as my personal memories unfold, but at least some attention must be given to it here, before I embark upon that kind of voyage.

Lovecraft was born at 454 Angell Street, the home of his maternal grandfather, on August 20, 1890. It was a stately house and he often referred to it in his letters as the old Phillips mansion on the Ancient Hill. The early years of his childhood were spent for the most part in the Phillips residence, although he and his parents sometimes stayed a few weeks with close friends, and he mentioned one visit to Fall River which seems to have occurred before he was five.

His parents—Sarah Phillips Lovecraft and Winfield Scott Lovecraft—had no other children. His father was a traveling salesman of English ancestry, and the family saw him seldom. It has been said that he never renounced his British citizenship, but I doubt if there is any way by which this could be verified. Winfield Lovecraft died when his son was very small, and thus HPL's formative years were influenced far more by his grandfather, for whom he always had the highest admiration and respect.

Although Lovecraft's mother was not a vain or self-centered

woman and was held in high esteem by her friends, she had a tendency to be over-protective, and there can be no question that she made her son feel like an invalid from an early age. Actually he was not an invalid at all, although at a certain period in his boyhood or early adolescence, he appears to have suffered from ill-health which necessitated his removal from school. But any evidence that he differed greatly from the most robust of youngsters is far from conclusive, apart from the fact that "robust" would have been meaningless in relation to HPL, for he was of the wiry, resilient type, with no outward appearance of possessing exceptionally good health.

Though it may be a departure from anything in Freud, I have often thought that an over-solicitous parent, for whom a child has the kind of respect which goes with the way HPL felt about family traditions, is in a position to exercise more influence on a child's view of himself than an ordinary parent under ordinary circumstances. So sensitive was Lovecraft to such traditions almost from birth, that I doubt whether the parental dominance factor entered into the matter at all.

HPL's mother died during the first year of my correspondence with him, when his adolescent years were quite far in the past. Not until we met in person did he discuss his childhood years with me, and extensive as our talks became, he never depicted himself as having been the "sickly," nervously high-strung child or youth that more than one recent biographical sketch has seemingly taken for granted. He did confess to having been a kind of "semi-invalid" during one period of his boyhood and occasionally would use that term in relation to all the years which had preceded his arrival in New York. But as soon as I met him, I think he knew that I would dismiss the extension of that term to include his present self as an absurdity, and much as that whimsical pretension may have pleased a particular side of his nature (which I shall discuss later at some length), he quickly abandoned it.

After the death of his mother, her place at the 598 Angell Street residence to which they had moved was taken by his two aunts, Lillian P. Clark and Annie E. Phillips Gamwell. Mrs. Clark was several years older than her sister and perhaps a bit more matronly in aspect, although that quality is difficult to associate with a woman who was extremely quick in her movements and quite fragile physically. Mrs.

Gamwell was much more social-minded, and perhaps was more outgoing in general, although both women possessed in common the quality of great kindliness. They were perhaps just a trifle over-protective (if one must use that term), but this was chiefly toward providing their nephew with every possible comfort and freedom from strain which they had the wisdom to realize is necessary to *any* writer if he is to do his best creative work without becoming sidetracked or tormented by distractions. I am quite certain they never actually "coddled" him or were as neurotically over-solicitous as his mother had been, or indeed that they did anything whatsoever to make him feel a "semi-invalid."

His decision to marry in March 1924 was incredibly impulsive, totally unexpected by his friends and correspondents, and it occurred after the briefest of courtships. He always insisted that he had been persuaded to leave Providence by the prospect of a new, but reasonably settled, kind of existence in New York City which would enable him to continue with his writing and make new contacts in a rewarding, leisurely manner. And despite all that has been said to the contrary, there was just enough adventurousness, even somewhat reckless daring, in HPL's nature to have made such a prospect far from lacking in appeal.

Although New York at first enchanted him, his sojourn (which lasted only until April 1926) quickly turned into a nightmare. He could not abide the crowds, the high-pressure activity, the feeling that he was adrift and cut off from virtually everything he most treasured. The actual deterioration of his marriage took place a little more slowly than his disillusionment with the city itself, for the person who now had become Mrs. Sonia Lovecraft, a divorcee of thirty-nine with a grown daughter, was a woman of great understanding and very much in love with him. But Sonia totally failed to comprehend that nothing which happened to HPL in New York could possibly transform him into a young, alert, and eminently successful wage-earner of the 1920s.

What Lovecraft missed most was his removal from all aspects of the past that were intimately associated with the city of his birth—not only with his ancestral heritage, but with every cherished memory that went back to his earliest childhood. No longer could he take long, solitary walks through the streets which he felt could be found only on the Ancient Hill; no longer could he watch the play of sunlight and shadow on ancient steeples and sequestered churchyards where "dead leaves whisper of departed days, longing for sights and sounds that are no more," or pause occasionally to pat a stray cat before returning home. (He was inordinately fond of cats, but paradoxically enough, did not regard them as in any way allied to the Black Arts, regardless of their color. There was also an abundance of stray cats in New York, of course, but few other compensations for all that he had lost by breaking so abruptly with the past.)

In one of HPL's best-known short stories, which appears to verge slightly upon the autobiographical, the central character is depicted not only as an outsider but as something of a monster. It apparently gave Lovecraft a kind of whimsically ironic pleasure to picture himself in this manner because his love for the past was so deep-seated and ineradicable that it embraced both the vistas of light and grace and loveliness, and the dark crypts below the earth which cannot be explored with artistic fidelity unless one assumes the identity of a tomb-dweller.

But at least in one respect HPL *was* an outsider—his kindliness and his ability to relate to others without the faintest trace of self-seeking were extraordinary. I have encountered not a few men and women who would have been incapable of any ego-bolstering meanness, but in Howard it seemed to go just a little beyond even that. It is hard to explain or analyze, but it was a difference which could be sensed by everyone who knew him.

A short while after his return to Providence his marriage was terminated by a quietly arranged divorce. No two people could have parted more amicably, and though the stated cause was "desertion," there can be no doubt that the excuse was a mutually agreed upon one to outwit the outrageously barbaric statutes pertaining to divorce in almost every state at that time.

During this period HPL now resided with Mrs. Clark at 10 Barnes Street and then in 1933 moved to his final home, a Georgian dwelling at 66 College Street. He returned to New York a half-dozen times, and ceased to be quite the hermit as he had been before his marriage. He journeyed to New Orleans and Charleston and other cities where nocturnal excursions into the past could be pursued in so variegated a way that his escape from Time's tyranny might be constantly reinforced by beckoning ghosts from earlier centuries. Weed-choked patio gardens hidden from view by rusting iron grill-work particularly fascinated him, as did unbroken rows of old houses with blankly-staring windows dating back to the seventeenth and eighteenth centuries.

Although Lovecraft was later to be haunted by a poverty even more extreme than he had endured toward the end of his New York years, he still possessed a dwindling inheritance which he managed to supplement by ghost-writing for eight or ten revision clients and through the occasional sale of a story. (During at least five years, story sales added considerably to his always small income, despite the low rate of payment which prevailed at the time.) This enabled him to avoid stripping his traveling expenses to a wholly fleshless kind of bone, an unpleasantness which can mar every planned excursion to some extent, even when it does not appreciably shorten it.

In outward appearance HPL remained unchanged even when he seemed to be journeying back through time, until the colonial period dimmed and vanished, and was replaced by a crowded Roman marketplace or a stone column close to the Forum. Poe's most striking feature, a forehead so high and broad it verged on the idiosyncratic, was not possessed by Lovecraft, who rather had a brow of moderate expanse. (I never asked him, but he was too well-versed in physiognomy on a sound scientific level to believe that such an incredible expanse of forehead had anything to do with Poe's intellectual endowments or his poetic genius, since it has been established beyond dispute that quite low brows are to be found in many men of genius and quite high ones are not at all unlikely in idiots.)

Below his brow, a nose (with perhaps just enough curvature to justify describing it as aquiline and a little on the bony side) and a rather elongated lower jaw gave him somewhat the aspect of a medieval scholar who has spent long hours poring over illuminated manuscripts, his features lengthening a little year by year until that prolonged concentration has caused him to blink more often than the unscholarly are ever likely to do, all apart from the eyestrain factor. It was an expressive, kindly face, the opposite of handsome, but animated by alert and perceptive eyes that occasionally could assume a look of piercing intensity.

During his periodic trips to New York he would sometimes bring his newest story with him and read it aloud while seated in a comfortable chair. Once in bleak midwinter before a crackling log fire, I was the first to hear *The Dunwich Horror*, *The Whisperer in Darkness*, and three or four other stories of novelette length, with their dramatization on the screen, radio, and television many years in the future.

Although he lacked an accomplished actor's stage presence, HPL was an extremely gifted mimic, and the change which came over him on these occasions was astounding. His voice deepened and became more resonant; as he entered his inner world of cosmic strangeness and alien dimensions, he became the protagonist of the story without ceasing to be H. P. Lovecraft. Despite its increased resonance, his voice never lost its conversational tone and never once verged on the oratorical (and that, in a way, made the entire recital more convincing). By combining the tone of a cultivated New Englander with the rustic accents of a fictional character of dark and terrifying antecedents, he created, particularly in *The Whisperer in Darkness,* a kind of paradoxical double image which made those readings unforgettable. He did not, of course, combine the two impressions in an overlapping way at any point in the story, but the overall impression still remained as I have described.

If HPL had written only stories of supernatural horror dealing with malign, tomb-dwelling presences of destructiveness and dread, his writing would nevertheless have challenged comparison with the best of Bierce, Blackwood, A. E. Coppard, M. R. James, Saki, and Walter de la Mare, to mention just six masters of the macabre among perhaps ten writers of comparable stature after Poe who excelled in that particular realm. But the cycle of stories which has become known as the Cthulhu Mythos not only sets Lovecraft apart from all other writers in the genre; it is simply without parallel in the whole of literature.

Recently described as "the myth that has captured a generation," the Mythos presents an entire pantheon of Elder Gods and of eon-banished entities which come terrifyingly to life through their unfolding genealogy. Long before the birth of the solar system, these "Old Ones" were cast into outer darkness by forces less powerful than themselves through a cataclysm of undreamed of violence, and someday they will awaken from slumber to reclaim the whole of their lost heritage, which includes the entire universe of stars. Already they have begun to stir and creep back into human consciousness in night-shadowed dreams of madness and death. Cthulhu, a creature of nightmare dimensions whom Lovecraft wisely chose not to describe beyond hinting that he was vaguely fishlike and terrible beyond belief, is the dominant entity in this cosmic assemblage. His frightfulness becomes wholly believable because HPL has succeeded in maintaining, in every story in the Mythos, the total "suspension of disbelief" that is the hallmark of truly imaginative myth-making.

There are few passages in the Mythos which afford the reader respite from the eerie forebodings that mount gradually to an awesome climax; nothing here in the least resembles that illusory calm in the midst of a hurricane which permits momentary self-deception. Instead, icy winds of horror blow inexorably with steadily increasing violence until all is engulfed in an amorphously swirling kind of vastness that topples cities and whips the sea into gigantic waves with an ominous warning impossible to ignore:

> Cthulhu still lives...again in that chasm of stone which has shielded him since the sun was young. His accursed city is sunken once more...but his ministers on earth still bellow and prance and slay around idol-capped monoliths in lonely places...Who knows the end? What has risen may sink and what has sunk may rise. Loathsomeness waits and dreams in the deep, and decay spreads over the tottering cities of men.

Although my own stories followed a somewhat different pattern in their approach to the macabre and were less cosmic even when exploring the mysteriously multidimensional aspects of Time and Space or the legend-haunted avenues of forgotten civilizations, it is not too surprising that one of these early tales, *The Hounds of Tindalos,* became incorporated into the Mythos. I have always felt it was an undeserved honor, but our long friendship made it more or less inevitable, particularly since the elaboration of his Mythos by others appealed irresistibly to the whimsical, boyish side of HPL's nature.

Robert Bloch, who was also an early correspondent, contributed several chilling entities, and so did Clark Ashton Smith and two other *Weird Tales* writers. In *The Shambler from the Stars,* written perhaps a year before its publication in *Weird Tales* in 1935, Bloch not only makes HPL the central character (very much as I did in *The Space Eaters*) but links the Old Ones to several wholly fiendish entities of his own creation to which HPL himself subsequently responded with a sequel!

Smith's Tsathoggua came closest to Cthulhu in frightfulness, but was otherwise quite different—a monstrous demon god not unlike those Indonesian effigies that adorn village huts, magnified a thousand times, and possessing far more inscrutable, universe-altering endowments. But he could ride comfortably, if hideously, on the cosmic winds generated by Cthulhu, and in all probability bowed to him as the Master.

My contributions to the Mythos were of assorted shapes and sizes, ranging from the tiny, flesh-devouring Doels, who inhabited an alien dimension shrouded in night and chaos, to the monstrous Chaugnar Faugn, whom only the suicidally inclined would have mistaken for a pachyderm. I also contributed one scenic vista, the mysterious, perpetually mist-shrouded Plateau of Leng, and one forbidden book, John Dee's English translation of *The Necronomicon,* which I placed at the head of *The Space Eaters* when that story first appeared in *Weird Tales,* but later omitted when the story was reprinted in *The Magazine of Horror,* fearing that my invention might take on an appalling life of its own and appear on the shelves of some unsuspecting and defenseless book dealer! (It has been rumored that the original Arabic text once thus materialized and only a mound of ashes was found between the book racks the following morning…)

HPL also incorporated into the Mythos more than one allusion to entities that Robert W. Chambers had depicted (with far less consideration for book dealers) in The King in Yellow, a theoretically non-existent volume having much in common with The Necronomicon. Virtually all myth cycles, fictional or otherwise, include these "fringe-level" borrowings, which but to a minor extent enter into the main body of the cycle. The contributions of other writers did not diminish the genius-inspired originality of the Cthulhu Mythos; in its major aspects it remains entirely Lovecraftian. But Lovecraft could take mythical names or references, sometimes tossed off without too much thought, and cloak them with an aura of awesome mystery. Conscious artifice of this nature had, I have always felt, no important bearing on the visions which Lovecraft could conjure up when he became wholly absorbed in his writing. Then his tremendous creativity took over, and mere artifice was swept aside by a total surrender to "dreams no mortal had ever dared to dream before." At such moments cities hoary with age, crumbling into ruin on the planet of some distant star, echoed to his footsteps, and it was easy to picture him bending to examine some instrument of nonhuman science, dating back ten billion years.

CHAPTER THREE

There can be no doubt whatsoever that HPL was quite different in many important ways from his grammar school classmates of seventy years ago. While every man of great imaginative brilliance has displayed enough unusual qualities in childhood to have drawn attention to himself at one time or another, Howard was a bit more than just a highly imaginative and sensitive child; he was a youthful prodigy who could compose rhymed verse at the age of six.

If he astonished his teachers by being able to converse with them quietly like a small adult, he must have astonished his classmates even more. As a rule, only a miracle can spare this type of child from the bullying tendencies which are the worst aspect of what happens when children of a dozen different family backgrounds and genetic endowments are thrown together in one school. But in HPL's case the miracle took place.

He often discussed his school days with me, and if any deep mental wounds with their residual scars had been inflicted upon him, the concealment of such wounds solely to spare himself painful memories would have been totally inconsistent with the candor which was as natural to him as breathing when he dwelt upon the past. The psychological trauma which Freud ascribes to buried childhood memories would have met a stumbling block straight off, if HPL had for a moment allowed himself to take psychoanalysis seriously. I doubt whether he had any buried memories at all that did not go back to his actual infancy, for from that period onward, every tormenting confrontation with reality he may have experienced would have remained for him indelibly inscribed as on the pages of an open book, readily accessible to total memory recall. And no psycho-therapeutic prodding would have been required to induce such a recollection.

There were two aspects of his character which were, I am convinced, as pronounced in him when he was very young as when I first met him. He possessed the sort of innate personal dignity and belief in himself that would have made a great many schoolboy bullies draw back, not always for ignoble reasons. Even the worst of bullies have a tendency, despite themselves, to respect this kind of high integrity. Howard also possessed indomitable personal courage. Any classroom bully who encroached to a serious extent on his right to prideful independence (and I can picture him as being compassionately tolerant of very minor infringements) would almost certainly have found himself confronting a detached, cool-tempered fighting machine that would have stretched him out on the floor in short order. Even if that particular bully had been ten pounds heavier with a longer reach, I am certain Howard would have prevailed with comparative ease.

Despite the "invalidism" which his mother's over-solicitude to some extent succeeded in inflicting upon him, HPL possessed a certain measure of physical strength. It was so much in evidence in his later years that it could hardly have been absent in a child who never set about building his muscles in a systematic way to compensate for a "frailness" which I doubt he ever took as seriously as some of his early correspondents probably believed.

Actually, there was nothing frail about him, even though he did not enjoy robust health at any time in his life. He was, of course, totally unlike the roaring, Falstaffian sort of literary hero with a bone-crushing handclasp which Hemingway preferred to regard as super-masculine. But very few sensitive, creative artists of any real achievement appear to have been that type, and the list includes Poe and Joyce and Yeats and even what little we know concerning the personal attributes of Shakespeare himself. (All of the portraits of the Bard of Avon, whether authentic or not, suggest that the poet was no more Hemingwayesque in aspect than Shelley or Keats or Santayana.)

During his formative years, HPL engaged in many of the hobbies and enthusiasms commonly associated with boyhood. At one time he was a member of an alert group of youngsters who had built up an impressive sleuthing apparatus modeled upon the Burns Detective Agency, which at the turn of the century was the only investigative bureau that had acquired so nationwide a reputation that every twelve year old in America was familiar with its slogan: "We always get our man." Or so Howard assured me, at least, since the agency was formed soon after the Civil War and thus preceded my birth by a few years! In any case, I was far too young to have been aware of what was taking place in that realm even as late as 1910, when Howard had long since abandoned his interest in becoming an early equivalent of Hammett's "Thin Man." At a somewhat earlier age when he was seven or eight, he joined some neighboring youngsters in forming a firefighting brigade which moved up and down the streets of the Ancient Hill with hook-and-ladder equipment of miniature size which they had managed to put together from wooden crates and garden hoses.

Very much on record in previous Arkham House books and elsewhere, is HPL's involvement with astronomy in his teenage years, leading to a column under his byline in the *Providence Evening Tribune* which one Providence elder refused to believe he could have authored, even when he produced a volume of cuttings (he always called them "cuttings," never "clippings") to prove it.

I do not know whether Howard ever engaged in that most universal of boyhood hobbies, stamp collecting, and my failure ever to ask him surprises me a little, because I was the most ardent of stamp collectors between the ages of nine and twelve. I do know that he collected coins, for in his New York period his knowledge of Roman numismatics was as extensive as his familiarity with ancient bronze and baked-clay Roman lamps, and he once helped me pick out magnificent examples of both "coinage and lampage" at an old-coin shop on Fulton Street. (I still possess a Roman silver coin as large as a fifty-cent piece, uneven about the edges, which I purchased on that occasion for the incredible sum of two dollars, but perhaps it is of some base alloy that merely looks like silver. I have never bitten into it to make sure.)

At the age of thirty, HPL's views in many areas would have stunned anyone unfamiliar with the New England character at its most puritanical. The image he had of himself was that of a man of stern moral principles, ultraconservative in outlook, and opposed to any kind of bohemianism. Yet this was precisely the opposite of a hypocritical self-image; holding such views seemed to him both natural and necessary, and entirely in accord with the code of a gentleman.

It seemingly cost him no apparent effort or misgivings to be that kind of a person. He not only would have failed to derive the slightest emotional satisfaction from going contrary to such a code, but would have felt he had betrayed the highest instincts of his being. Howard believed there was nothing in that code which could keep a man from being both poet and dreamer, or from admiring the best that has been said and thought in the world. In the realm of aesthetics, the great poets meant as much to him as they did to me, and although out of fealty to his beloved eighteenth century he preferred Pope and Dryden to Keats and Shelley, he would instantly have conceded that the major romantic poets, from Coleridge to Swinburne, were of considerably greater stature.

Before concluding the somewhat statistical aspects of this record and passing on to personal memories, there is a matter of great importance which the reader must constantly keep in mind, or otherwise the way HPL refers to himself in many of the conversations which follow will seem bewildering and difficult to understand. I am uncertain precisely when Howard became convinced that he was "the old gentleman from Providence-Plantations," but I strongly suspect the feeling that he was at least two and a half times his calendar age first began to take shape in his mind before he was twenty-five. I only know that when he arrived in New York it had become so settled a conviction that he referred to me and to his other young correspondent, Alfred Galpin, as his "grandsons"; to James F. Morton, who was just as much of an inner-circle correspondent and was almost twice his age, as "my son"; and to one of his aunts, Mrs. Gamwell, as "my daughter."

He sometimes spoke of me as "Sonny"—a designation which I found provoking, but since he more often addressed me as "Belknapius," (My middle name was used by my family to distinguish me from my father since I was a "Jr.") I did not wish to offend him by protesting too vigorously whenever he engaged in that silly-sounding lapse, which he seemed unable totally to avoid. I did protest once or twice, but it did no good. He went right on calling me "Sonny" in an occasional letter and more often in his communications to others until I began to feel, at thirty or so, that the absurdity of it exceeded all bounds. No one had ever called me "Sonny" before—even at the age of fifteen—because all apart from its juvenile implications, the name suggests a buoyant, cheerful, jack-in-the-box disposition which I emphatically never possessed. But it was impossible to stay angry with

HPL for long, and since I am certain he would have dropped the appellation instantly and forever had I been sufficiently insistent in my protests, I have only myself to blame for what would have become even more of an absurdity if at my present age of a hundred and ten, he could have continued to address me—if only on rare occasions—as the "Sonny" of that long vanished segment of Space and Time.

CHAPTER FOUR

I might never have met HPL had I not entered an essay contest conducted by a magazine which I believe was called *Boys' World.* I won first prize and Paul Campbell, a wildcat oil well promoter residing in the Southwest, saw the story and invited me to join the United Amateur Press Association.

Campbell was not just an oil well promoter. He was a widely read man of scholarly tastes, and the United Amateur Press Association, along with the National Amateur Press Association, occupied a unique role in the early development of small, privately owned presses not too different from the present-day ones which are everlastingly in motion turning out science fiction and fantasy fan magazines from coast to coast.

I immediately enrolled in the UAPA, and a short while later my first published story, *The Eye Above the Mantel,* appeared in *The United Amateur,* the association's official journal. As a member of this organization, HPL saw the story and wrote me a quite long letter about it. Although it was written on a penny postal, the calligraphy was so minute that it must have run almost to the equivalent of two manuscript pages, so "quite long letter" is not a misnomer.

He praised the story highly, and I have sometimes let myself believe that the praise was not *wholly* undeserved, because it was one of those freak occurrences which can only happen to the very young, who come so totally under the spell of a writer of genius at times that they are seized by an imitative exuberance which results in something a little on the special side. It was wholly imitative, and I had followed, in an almost slavish way, in the footsteps of a master—and that master happened to be Edgar Allan Poe.

The story was so much like Poe's *Shadow—A Parable* in the cadenced solemnity of its prose, that it could probably have passed for an undiscovered story by this author. I think it could have gotten by as such, because it was just different enough from the *Shadow* to give it the appearance of not having been inked out, phrase by phrase, on a sheet of transparent tracing paper.

At least Howard liked it, and we started a correspondence that must have run to fifty letters in a two-way exchange until that day in April 1922 when I answered the phone and discovered that HPL was in New York, no further away from my Manhattan address at the time than the Prospect Park's Flatbush-encroaching extremity.

"Belknapius?" he asked. It would probably have been: "Hello. May I speak to Mr. Long, please?" if the youthful tone of my voice had not made it seem unlikely that it could have been my father, who had a very brisk, professional-sounding voice as well. Howard had never heard him speak, but I am quite certain my voice, then as now, does not conjure up visions of a cool, efficient surgeon-dentist pausing in the midst of a tooth extraction to answer the telephone. And HPL was extremely perceptive about the kind of voice he correctly attributed to the majority of men who deal with emergencies on any level, and who lack the outward exuberance of a free-wheeling young imaginative fiction writer.

On that particular morning I had been reading a book that had greatly enchanted me, and would have answered any phone call in the same exuberant manner, even if it had been a call from our local grocer. Curiously enough, my memory of what HPL said on the wire during the ensuing conversation remains on the almost total recall level. I can remember him saying, with amusing formality: "This is Howard Phillips Lovecraft."

And I think I said: "Well, I'll be damned!" or "This is terrific!" or something of the sort. "Where are you phoning from?"

"I'm at Mrs. Greene's home in Brooklyn," he said. "It's very far out, on Parkside Avenue. She invited me to be her guest for a few days."

There was a long pause before he continued. "As I believe I mentioned briefly in one of my letters, we met last year at a Boston convention. She's a very prominent amateur journalist and publishes and edits a magazine of her own—*The Rainbow*. I intended to send you a copy, but now that won't be necessary. You'll be impressed when you see it."

There was another pause before he continued. "I must confess I didn't expect to meet anyone at the convention *quite* so congenial. We have a great many interests in common, and she seems able to ignore the reserve which has sometimes been attributed to me, probably justly, since I'm so much the opposite of a well-traveled person and feel just a little ill at ease in gatherings of this nature. She made me forget my years whenever we engaged in conversation. I've never felt capable of forgetting my age for very long, and I'm afraid I've never wanted to be thought of as the kind of impetuous elderly gentleman who allows himself to be flattered when such a mistake is made by an attractive young lady."

The phone conversation was not interrupted at this point by yet another pause, but for a moment so many incredible thoughts were passing through my mind that I failed to pay strict attention to what he was saying.

At that time Howard was only thirty-two and Sonia was seven years older—and he had mentioned her age in his letter! But it was not in the least unusual for anyone, elderly or otherwise, to refer to a woman of thirty-nine as an "attractive young lady." Young as I was in the early 1920s, that sort of gallantry was so common that I occasionally found myself thinking of stunningly beautiful women older than Sonia in precisely that way—and not always out of gallantry. This did not mean I was attracted more by older women than by younger ones, but to me a stunningly beautiful woman has always seemed ageless.

No—it was not that which set my thoughts whirling, for by this time I was thoroughly familiar through our correspondence with Howard's "old gentleman" pretense. What seemed incredible to me was the indisputable fact that Howard, despite his puritanical scruples, had become the invited guest of an "unchaperoned" young lady at her Brooklyn apartment!

I had no way of knowing that she was "unchaperoned," but the assumption seemed warranted somehow, and when one jumps to that kind of conclusion it can sometimes carry as much conviction as an established fact. If I had paid just a little more attention to his words at this point, enlightenment would have come more quickly than it did. But it came quickly enough.

"Samuelus is sharing the apartment with me, and Sonia is staying with a neighbor in another apartment on the same floor. He's also here on a temporary visit, to explore some employment prospects which Sonia feels should be looked into. He has been planning to leave Cleveland—he isn't as attached to that burg as I am to Providence—and settle in New York permanently. It would be a very sensible move and I've told him so."

I had never met Samuel Loveman, but Howard had corresponded with him for several years. Since there was no amateur journalist whose name HPL failed to Latinize after the exchange of several letters, the "Samuelus" did not surprise me. At that time I knew of Loveman only as a gifted young poet, although for Howard he had attained the extremely advanced age which sets a man in his middle thirties quite apart from such youngsters as myself.

Howard was talking very rapidly now.

"Why don't you come over! Samuelus is out now, making an inspection tour of Prospect Park. But he'll be back in time for dinner. Sonia is doing some shopping and also some marketing, in preparation for a five-course meal that she may feel has gone unappreciated when she glances at my platter. The old gentleman eats sparingly at all times. But Samuelus has a hearty appetite and consumes nearly everything that is placed before him. I encourage him in this, and hope that Sonia will not notice how much food goes back to the kitchen unconsumed. Her cooking is so excellent and she devotes so much time to the preparation of a meal that I try to make up for what I lack in gustatory appreciation with the most effusive kind of praise. Effusive it may be, but that does not mean that it is not sincere. But you will soon discover for yourself what a superb cook she is."

Quite obviously Howard was not the kind of man a woman could hope to ensorcell through her culinary gifts alone!

Although I did not pause in my reply, I must do so here to elaborate a bit on what passed through my mind when he informed me without preamble that he had become the guest of a woman he had only recently met. Such thoughts had occurred to me only because he had made clear in his letters exactly how he felt about the setting aside of all conventional attitudes in the realm of sex. What Calvin Coolidge once said about sin, "I am not for it," would have been just as applicable to the way Howard felt about what has sometimes been called a Victorian hangup in that particular realm. Only with Howard, it was not precisely a hangup.

Actually Howard had no hangups whatsoever in a strict sense, because his standards of deportment were basic to his very nature.

Puritan traditions he respected and adhered to, but the prudish trappings of Victorian convention he regarded as quite laughable—at least insofar as they were prudish. When Victorian conventions were completely in accord with his inner convictions, defying them would have made no sense to him. But in his correspondence he made his dislike for the entire Victorian era—including its residual spillover in America as late as the early 1920s—so unmistakably plain that my testimony is not needed to confirm it. It is too much a matter of firmly established biographical record.

But I was not concerned with such matters that morning, for they had little to do with HPL's totally unexpected phone call.

"I'll start right off," I told him. "I should be there in about one hour."

"Sonia's out now, as I've said, but she'll be back well before two-thirty at the latest. She's looking forward to meeting you," he added. "She's read two of your stories."

"I hope you didn't talk her into liking them, against her better judgment."

"There was no need. She thought they were splendid," Howard said, and then continued: "She has a daughter about your age. I was careful not to tell her I have two grandsons who have the foolish idea they are young Casanovas."

"I'll be careful to give her the contrary impression," I assured him. "That's not such a good idea with some girls, though. Is she stunningly beautiful?"

"What a decadent generation this is! Is that the first thing you think about when you meet a very sensible, attractive young lady?"

I had not intended to end that phone call on a note of levity. But HPL had surprised me a little by engaging in the amiable sort of chiding which up to that time was of fairly rare occurrence in his letters. One never knows anyone well until one has met him in person, and from that moment his correspondence will often take on a more exuberant kind of informality.

Parkside Avenue is far out in Brooklyn, almost as far as the more distant regions of historic Flatbush and the sea-bright traceries of Coney Island which never fail to bring to mind some New England seacoast town. I have never otherwise cared too much for Brooklyn, but have always preferred it to the vast, sprawling wasteland of the

Bronx, where there is little of an associational nature that appeals to me. Just the thought of meeting HPL for the first time, however, blurred all distinctions between the boroughs.

Sonia resided in a four room, first floor apartment in a red brick building not more than four stories in height, and Howard was sitting on one of the two stone walls that ran from the entrance to the street and enclosed a small garden of flowering plants.

As I approached the apartment house there was no one else in sight, and I was certain it was HPL even before I was close enough to recognize him from the two photographs he had sent me. At that time he had grown quite stout, for a normally lean man about five-eleven in height. (He often referred to his weight at that period as ridiculous and was glad that he had succeeded in becoming lean again some two years later.) He looked a great deal older than thirty-two, and his rather settled, fortyish aspect struck me as at least more in accord with his "elderly gentleman" pretense than the distinctly collegiate look which not a few men manage to retain until the onset of middle age.

It was only when he rose and grasped my hand in greeting that I realized there was still a certain boyishness about him that could not be concealed. It was particularly noticeable in the region of his eyes, and his voice was not that of a middle-aged man.

"Belknapius!" he said, quite simply, just as he had done on the phone. "Well...*well!* You look just as I thought you would." He paused to pass his hand across his brow. "I guess we'd better get away from this glare. Soaking up the sun's rays to saturation point is just what my old bones need. But I've been sitting here reading for half an hour and it has given me a slight headache. Sonia thinks I should wear reading glasses, but I hate the feel of them on my nose. I'll wait a few more years, when I'll probably go stumbling around anyway." (He had worn glasses once, I remembered, from the first photograph of him I had ever seen, but I did not remind him of that.)

I wish I could say that the book he had just set down on the red brick neo-Colonial wall was some forbidden volume hoary with age, dating back at least to Nyarlathotep's Cthulhu-contending reign. But unhappily it was leather bound and as modern looking as the wall—a guidebook to the historical antiquities of Brooklyn which Sonia had recently given him.

"We may as well go inside," he reiterated, gesturing toward the apartment house entrance, which had a coolly inviting look. "Sonia was delighted when I told her Parkside Avenue was just a stone's throw away to you…"

"I never seem able to keep an appointment on time," he added, self-castigatingly. "Usually I'm a half-hour late—or more." (He could sometimes be two hours late, as I discovered subsequently when his failure to arrive at the American Museum of Natural History at an early hour in the afternoon forced me to phone him twice, and despair of seeing him before the shadows lengthened in the Hall of Man and made the glass-encased, fossilized skulls assume a more ominous aspect.)

"I've never been able to rush," he said. "It makes some people here justifiably angry and it's something I'll have to remedy. But long-established habits are difficult to overcome when you've been so long out of touch with the rushing about people can't seem to avoid in a city like New York. No one in Providence would think of rushing so much—at least, no one on the Hill. Boston is bad enough in that respect, but New York—"

"You get accustomed to it," I said. "I don't like it any more than you do. But there are some things you have to take in stride, or the enormity of having everyone go into a rage will begin to wear on your nerves."

"Some people take offense so easily—and for trivial reasons," he said. "But I know that my lateness is not trivial, and I'll have to make more of an effort to get to places on time."

"What did you think of the Manhattan skyline?" I asked. It was the most trite of the many unnecessary questions which visitors from elsewhere have to endure. But I really wanted to know.

"I've seen it before, in some of my earliest dreams," he said. "When I first read the *Arabian Nights* I was sure that pinnacles so shiningly splendid had to exist somewhere. And that made me see them, almost as they are. The reality is just a little more breathtaking, but the very shape of many of the towers against the sky is no different from the way they looked when I just shut my eyes and tried to recapture what I'd seen in dreams. I usually succeeded so well that the skyline brought back a feeling of familiarity when I saw it from the train window for the first time."

"It's not exactly Arabian," I said.

"But that's just it. It's *fabulously* Arabian, in a superior way. More magnificent, more strange than any Middle Eastern skyline could possibly be. But oriental notwithstanding. It would have widened the eyes of a desert wayfarer, I'm sure, even without a jinni towering over it. I could have seen a jinni with very little additional effort. But it wasn't necessary for me to conjure one up."

"Well I suppose you could say all that about it," I conceded. "But to a native-born New Yorker it doesn't have quite that kind of associational aspect. It even depresses me a little at times, because it dwarfs the individual so much. When I think of all that massed impersonal wealth and power, my identity as an individual has a tendency to shrivel to the dimensions of a gnat."

"I don't give that part of it a thought," Howard said. "I can separate the things that please me from this decadent industrial age. In Prospect Park and in what little I've seen of Manhattan there are scenic vistas of pure enchantment. White stone pillars and weaving boughs against a sunset sky—elm-shaded streets that could just as easily be in Providence, with just as many Georgian houses that have defied the years."

If the conversation I am quoting seems distinctly long-winded and rather remote from the pleasure he had clearly experienced on greeting me in person for the first time, it was no different from the manner Howard usually spoke when he was carried away by anything that enabled him to travel into the past on monorails of his own imagination. And my question had provided him with an opportunity to do just that, despite his stated intention to retreat indoors from the glaring sun.

"I caught just a glimpse of those streets when we arrived yesterday, before we descended into the subway," he went on, after a pause. "The photographs in the guidebooks I studied don't begin to do them justice. Street after street of dwellings virtually unchanged, with no new, ugly buildings towering over them as they do further uptown. Nothing but small-paned windows and fan-lighted doorways greeted my ancient eyes for ten or twelve blocks."

I very much wanted to meet Sonia. But I felt that if I remained silent and looked a little unhappy, the sun glare would get to him again. He had begun to blink and suddenly he was gesturing toward the apartment entrance for the second time.

"Well, we'd better go inside," he said. "My eyes seldom give me any trouble. But today I don't know—the sun's hot enough to burn holes in the pavement, so I suppose that has something to do with it."

The apartment looked just as I had imagined it would—modest but very tastefully furnished, with some interesting family portraits on the walls. Sonia was not in the living room, but I could hear her moving about in either the adjoining room or kitchen. A faint clattering sound, as if a cup or spoon had just been set down, suggested that it was probably the kitchen.

I sat down on a sofa by the window and we talked for perhaps ten or fifteen minutes longer. Then Howard vanished for an instant, and when he reappeared he was accompanied by Sonia. She was still wearing a sun-shielding straw hat and was attired in a simple print dress that set off her dark beauty in an extremely becoming way. She was far more attractive than I had thought she might be, for her amateur journalism activities alone could have made Howard overlook plainness in a woman who was able to convince him that they had many interests in common.

She came straight toward me across the room, smiling graciously, and I seem to recall that I was the first to extend my hand—an inexcusable lapse of etiquette which I doubt if I shall ever be able to overcome on rare occasions, when self-consciousness makes me unable to avoid a reflex action of that kind.

"Belknapius," she said, taking my hand and warmly pressing it. "Howard has told me all about you. His other grandson, Alfred Galpin, I met last year. He looks just a little older than you do, but I guess that's because he's read Nietzsche."

"I've read Nietzsche too," I said. "Is that supposed to age you beyond your years?"

"Sonia thinks so," Howard said. "Alfredus wrote an article about him for *The Rainbow* that she finds it hard to believe could have been written by anyone younger than thirty-five or forty. Even by someone the same age as the old gentleman."

"Old gentleman!" Sonia said. "Did he always write about himself in that way in his letters to you?"

"I'm afraid so," I told her.

"Well, he's got to get over that. It's just plain silly."

"She knows how old I am," Howard said. "Thirty-two can be quite an advanced age if you're born aged."

"He was no different from other children," Sonia said. "I know, because both of his aunts told me he could go into temper tantrums and make as much trouble for people as any other perfectly normal, sweet little child."

It was at this point that something which at first had been a mere suspicion began to lodge itself more firmly in my mind. During the brief talk by the window Howard had dwelt at some length on Sonia's meeting with his aunts and on two other occasions when they had spent considerable time together on New England terrain, with the Boston convention several weeks in the past.

Could it be possible—It *was* possible, of course, and if Howard's phone call had not made everything else seem of lesser importance than meeting him in person for the first time, I would have realized sooner that his relationship with Sonia had taken on what could only be thought of as a just-short-of-engagement character. It still was only at the friendship stage perhaps, but with the distinct possibility that it might soon become something more.

What she had just said went a long way toward confirming this, for she had assumed a kind of proprietorship over his childhood years, as if reliving them with him might well become an almost daily occurrence in the years ahead. And the instant Howard had returned into the room with Sonia at his side, I could not dismiss the feeling that he was perfectly willing to have her regard him as just a little more than a temporary—if cordially welcomed—guest. Temporary on that particular occasion, of course. But occasions of that nature can very quickly undergo a change.

The change was less swift than it might have been, for it took almost two years for the accuracy of my surmise to be confirmed in every respect. But in a letter to his aunts written shortly after his return to New York as a married man, he confessed that it could—and should—have happened at an earlier date and only his extreme conservatism had led him to put it off, a fault which Sonia had graciously forgiven, but which he found it hard to forgive in himself.

Sonia was an extraordinarily attractive woman, of such striking dark beauty that it would have made her stand out in a social gathering with at least four or five only slightly less attractive competitors drifting about. I am not exaggerating here. Although she was thirty-nine at the time, she did not appear a day older than Howard's actual age, and about thirty years younger than the fictitious age which he agreed was peculiar to himself, perhaps, but which could not be brushed off as lightly as she had just attempted to do.

She was of Jewish ancestry and Russian-born. There was a very competent, practical side to her nature, and she had a lively sense of humor and a keenly observant mind. But despite her success as a millinery shop executive in the early 1920s, she was not in any basic way a worldly-minded or very sophisticated woman. She at times could be quite sentimental to an utterly naive extent, a trait of course which was not at all shared by Howard. But she had several qualities in common with him, not the least of which was a puritanical bias almost as pronounced as his own. I have often thought this may have been the quality which most appealed to him when they met in Boston for the first time. The four qualities which seem to me today to have been most pronounced in Sonia were kindliness, warmth, generosity, and graciousness. And if there are any more admirable qualities—apart from high artistic achievement which is on another plane—they have so far escaped my notice.

Sonia could sometimes dramatize some particular event in her life out of all reason, in a wholly melodramatic way. I am indebted to Alfred Galpin for the following amusing story, which she related to him when they met in Madison, Wisconsin the year before.

When she was in her early twenties a young admirer succeeded in convincing himself that her virtue was not unassailable. When she invited him to her home following a theater engagement for a cup of Russian tea, he made a daring proposal, with seduction uppermost in his mind. She had just turned from the window after throwing the casement wide, and the apartment was several stories above the street.

Her immediate response was: "Ivan Ivanowich"—or whatever his name was!—"if you take one step nearer I shall hurl myself from this window!"

I have never doubted that she might well have carried out the threat, and one can readily imagine into what a state of agitation that particular suitor must have been plunged. Allowance must be made, of course, for the sort of wildly melodramatic behavior that appears to have been far more common at one time in continental Europe than it has ever been in America, and the fact that Sonia had spent her childhood in Russia and had not arrived in the United States before the age of eight or ten.

I cannot quite recall what we talked about for the remainder of that afternoon. I do remember leafing through *The Rainbow* and admiring its distinct literary flavor—it was a quite exceptional amateur journalism magazine—and I am certain we discussed Howard's stories. I probably also quoted at least a hundred lines of Swinburne, since at that period I could seldom resist letting those wonderful, alliterative lines roll over me in great oceanic waves.

Then Loveman and Sonia's daughter returned from opposite ends of the Brooklyn compass at about the same time, and we sat around a long table while Sonia placed before us the kind of banquet Howard had mentioned over the phone. Sonia's daughter was very pretty, with freckles that met across the bridge of her nose, and blonde hair and a waist so slim it seemed a little unreal. Unfortunately she was soon to leave New York, to be with a young man to whom she had recently become engaged.

When Howard returned to the city again Sonia invited all of his friends who were in New York at the time to a Park-side Avenue housewarming that did not terminate until the early morning hours. Just who those friends were the next chapter will disclose.

CHAPTER FIVE

The Kalem Club derived its title from the fact that all of the early members had surnames beginning with K, L, or M—Morton, Kleiner, Kirk, Leeds, Loveman, McNeil, Long, and HPL himself. It existed in a very loosely-knit form several months before Howard's arrival in New York, for the members all knew each other through correspondence with Howard, and there had been several small gatherings at which three or four of them were present. I believe it was Rheinhart Kleiner who suggested the name and held the initial meeting at his Brooklyn home, but I am not certain of this since I was not present at what may have been the first time several of HPL's New York friends assembled in forum fashion.

Since references to the Kalem Club will occur throughout the following pages, a brief biographical sketch of each member becomes absolutely mandatory. (Even if it were not mandatory, I should like very much to run each sketch to a much greater length, but that must be ruled out or this would cease to be a memoir devoted primarily to HPL and his writings.)

James F. Morton corresponded voluminously with Howard for many years, and they met perhaps thirty times in person apart from the Kalem Club gatherings. I accompanied Howard twice on a visit to Paterson, New Jersey, after Morton had become the curator of the museum there; he joined us on a visit to the Poe cottage at Fordham and on a half-dozen other trips about New York, and also on a boat excursion from Providence to Newport several years later. With the exception of Everett McNeil, Morton was the oldest member of the Kalem group, just approaching fifty when Howard arrived in New York. Like Howard, however, he seemed ten years older than his actual age, for he wore his hair longish and had a somewhat patriarchal aspect, despite his great vigor and the youthful exuberance that he often displayed. Howard could manifest the same kind of exuberance, of course, which totally belied his elderly gentleman pretense.

Morton was a fabulous individual in many ways. He had a Harvard MA (at that time it was customarily called an AM, and carried more prestige than a PhD does today) and had somehow at the age of forty managed to get himself into *Who's Who in America*. He was a pioneer in the negro rights movement and lived in Harlem in an ancient brown-stone owned by a wealthy friend who shared his feelings about the outrageous discrimination which blacks had to endure in the 1920s. In his youth he had known and corresponded with Jack London, and at that time was a lecturer for the New York Board of Education. He supplemented his rather meager income by giving other lectures, and presided at all the meetings of the once famous Sunrise Club, as well as at the Blue Pencil Club, a Brooklyn-based amateur journalism group which Howard often attended as honorary member.

Because of his many and varied socio-political activities, Morton achieved considerable newspaper publicity and in a general way was considered at the time to be a quite prominent New Yorker. But again, like Howard, he was seldom free from economic strain and uncertainty until he secured the Paterson Museum sinecure. (Since most dictionaries define "sinecure" as a position that requires no work yet provides compensation, I have not chosen the right word, I fear. Morton was wholly dedicated to his museum duties and spent most of his weekends collecting minerals in the hills and valleys surrounding Paterson. The museum's collection soon became one of the finest in the eastern United States.)

If Charles Lamb could have been reincarnated as a New Yorker of the 1920 era, he might well have seemed little different from Rheinhart Kleiner, who as his name implies was of Germanic extraction. Lamb was not of Germanic extraction, of course, nor did he quite have Kleiner's constant eye for the ladies (to the exclusion, at times, of almost everything else); but both men were rather unworldly, almost gentle bookkeepers, and brilliant, enchantingly urbane poets. Kleiner's penchant for light verse was almost the exact equivalent of Lamb's equally light essays, except in the actual form in which they were cast.

Samuel Loveman hardly needs a sketch of more than a paragraph in length, because there can be few Lovecraftians who are unfamiliar with his poetic achievements, his early friendship with Bierce (Samuel Loveman, ed., *Twenty-one Letters of Ambrose Bierce* [Cleveland:

G. Kirk, 1922], and his long association and almost continuous correspondence with HPL. Many readers of this book will be familiar with his poems, for they have cast resplendent glimmerings upon the many-channeled stream of twentieth century poetry, despite a lack of widespread literary recognition in recent years. Bierce, Sterling, and Robinson Jeffers all knew how line his best poems were, and though only one slim volume bearing the Caxton Press imprint ever brought him critical praise, that volume is unique of its kind. Several years ago he appeared with Waldo Frank and three other friends of Hart Crane in a memorial tribute on New York's Channel 13 that brought back a memorable moment of HPL's New York years for me. Though HPL did not know Crane nearly as well as Loveman did, he met and talked with him several times, and one of those meetings at which I was also present seemed so prophetic of the fame that would overtake both writers that I recorded it in the 1944 Arkham House volume, *Marginalia*.

George Kirk was one of Loveman's early Cleveland friends, and a rare book dealer by profession who became a permanent New York resident at about the same time that Loveman did. His Chelsea Book Shop on Eighth Street in the Village was for many years a gathering place for the writers, editors, and publishers for whom the Village, in those far-off days, had something very special about it which it has largely lost today.

Arthur Leeds was a writer of perhaps forty-five—I am uncertain as to his exact age at the time—who was always under more of an economic strain than any other member of the group, not even excepting HPL. What saved him from utter destitution was the column he wrote for the *Writer's Digest,* "Thinks and Things"; his occasional sale of short stories to magazines such as *Adventure;* and his later employment as a staff worker at the midtown offices of the WPA Federal Writers Project. He was of Irish ancestry and took great pride in the fact that there were coats of arms on all four sides of his family. He was a cultivated and extremely likeable man, except when he succumbed to quite violent outbursts of rage. But that did not diminish Howard's liking and respect for him.

Everett McNeil was a writer of boys' books who resided in Hell's Kitchen in a small flat at the top of what seemed to be at least fifty flights of stairs. He was very much a recluse—white-haired, and so kindly disposed and forgiving toward everyone that even Howard had to caution him at times to exercise more severity toward editors who were unconscionably slow in reporting on manuscripts or in sending him desperately needed checks.

There was another member of the Lovecraft Circle who remained in New York only two days upon his return to America from overseas. He was not a member of the Kalem Club, and Howard was no longer in New York when I met him in person for the first time, after exchanging at least 200 letters. But Howard had previously met him in Cleveland and they had exchanged just as many letters, and he is so much a part of the memories which cluster about the early New York period that the previous sketches would be incomplete if I did not include a few paragraphs about Alfred Galpin.

Galpin was the earlier of the two adopted "grandsons" whom Howard mentioned often in his letters of that period. The other was myself. He once said that Galpin was the most brilliant of his several young correspondents, and I have always been in complete agreement with that appraisal. I have also felt that if Galpin had not turned from literature to music in his early twenties, and then to teaching (but without abandoning music), he would be today one of the foremost literary critics in America. But the choice was certainly his to make, and it seems to have enabled him to attain a richly rewarding kind of personal fulfillment which he perhaps could not have achieved in any other way. He has had an outstanding career as a teacher at the University of Wisconsin, and I have been told by a musician of major stature that the best of AG's compositions are genius-inspired.

When Galpin returned from Paris his attractive first wife, Lee, was present to meet him. They had only been married for a few months, and were as caught up in a mad kind of infatuation as I have ever known two people to be. Lee was staying at our home as a guest, for a telegram from Alfred had advised her as to the exact hour of the ship's arrival and she had arrived from Chicago a little ahead of time. Alfred returned wearing a long black cape and carrying a smuggled-in copy of *Ulysses*—the first edition, which would fetch an astronomical sum today.

Another member of the Lovecraft Circle who later became one of HPL's grandsons and who certainly, across the years, acquired memories of both Howard and the Circle that could easily run to several volumes of personal reminiscences of the most detailed character, was Donald Wandrei. My friendship with Donald goes back a great many years, and elsewhere I have discussed the monthly gatherings at which he presided during the period when he lived in the Village.

Hence no Wandrei sketch is needed here, but he remains just as closely associated with the early Kalem Club gatherings and with Howard's New York period in a symbolical way as does Alfred Galpin, although he did not live in New York until quite a few years later and did not then meet all of "the gang." When Donald first arrived in New York in 1927 he was only nineteen; a day or so later he traveled to Providence where he met both HPL and Morton, with the Long family following by car a few days after I had seen him off at the train. But the earlier Donald of those far-off days remains so closely linked to all of the associations which led to Howard's emergence from his Providence hermitage in the early 1920s that he remains in my mind in a separate compartment from the Donald of later years, who returned to St. Paul before coming to New York for the second time to acquire a position at E. P. Dutton and Company which was remarkably prestigious for a man in his early twenties.

The earlier Donald was very tall. He has always remained the same height, of course, but his tallness then seemed accentuated by his leanness! At that time he was much more broodingly introspective than talkative, and scarcely said a word on a ferry excursion from Battery Park to Staten Island which we took on the first day of his arrival. He simply stood on the upper deck staring out across the shining waters of the New York harbor with the poems he had recently written—and remarkable poems they were—protruding from his pocket.

This memoir would be incomplete if it failed to include a sketch of the author, and making that sketch just a bit longer than the previous ones can be justified, I think, without introducing the kind of apologies which are often advanced as the reason for such an exercise. It has nothing whatever to do with egoism or the lack of it. The reasons are as simple as they are unarguable: One—a memoir in which nothing whatever is revealed about the author's antecedents, his philosophical views, and his target-area visibility as an individual in relation to others, would be completely lopsided. It would fail to enable the reader to stand off and view him completely within target range, just as exposed as the subject of the memoir; and if what he has written seems unjustified or distorted, they will at least know that they are taking aim in the right direction with a fair chance of exacting retribution. Two—a portrait of someone one has known from birth, inside and out, can hardly fail to be of an enlivening nature, and when an opportunity for such three-dimensional portraiture presents itself, it would be a mistake to ignore it entirely.

My family background in general was not very different from HPL's. It was entirely New England on my mother's side, old New York on my father's. But there are historical associations relating to four of my ancestors, two direct and two collateral, which verge on the extraordinary in a colorful, contrasting manner.

One was of high estate but unquestionably an outright rogue: the Belknap who was the only American officeholder of cabinet rank ever to be impeached, a short while after the Civil War. (I am uncertain of the precise date for I have never looked it up, and not because he was a scoundrel. It just never seemed to me of great importance.) It was undoubtedly from him that I have inherited the disreputable side of my character. Or perhaps it was from Edward Doty, a direct maternal ancestor who was probably the only genuine non-Puritan on the *Mayflower,* a young lad from London Towne who was indentured to a Pilgrim family, had thirteen children, was put in the stocks, and was the first man to fight a duel on the American continent. I did not know that the Pilgrims fought duels until my mother showed me the Doty genealogy book—a huge volume bound in cloth, the family data assembled with brief biographical notes by my great grandfather—and there it was in black and white. (I believe there is a copy at the Forty-second Street Library, in one of the many fire-proof rooms given over to genealogy, but I have never looked that up either. The family volume has vanished with the years.)

But I do have more readily authenticated data concerning General Mansfield, who was the only general to die in battle in the War between the States. (He was shot from his horse at the battle of Antietam; it has always seemed enormously to his credit that he went right in with his men and took that much of a gamble.) The famous Civil War photograph of Lincoln with all the Northern generals in a battle tent setting shows my great uncle far off to the left, a slight figure below medium height. The other generals were listed by name when that photograph was published years ago in the *New York World*—not, of course, for the first time—but General Mansfield was referred to as "an unknown general." My aunt indignantly wrote a letter to the *World* about this, supplying some documentary evidence in her possession. I still have the yellowed clipping.

I have a great deal more authenticated material concerning my paternal grandfather, Charles O. Long, a building contractor. He erected the pedestal to the Statue of Liberty and was superintendent of the statue for several years before the government took over its administration from New York City. My father once possessed the French and American flags that were draped over the torch at the unveiling, and there was a full-page illustrated article about this in the *New York World-Telegram* some thirty-five years ago. I still possess an unveiling ceremony volume inscribed to my grandfather, bearing the signatures of several civil and military dignitaries, including the infamous General Butler, whose name cannot be mentioned in New Orleans even today without provoking outbursts of unrestrained rage. Pasted to the inner cover of that volume is another yellowed newspaper clipping dating back to the turn of the century: "Liberty's Guardian Dead."

One naturally takes a great deal of interest in his more immediate ancestry. But unlike HPL I never could summon up sufficient interest in remote family-tree relationships to uncover one-tenth as much about my ancestry as I might have done had I possessed James F. Morton's curiosity in that area. Morton's grandfather wrote "My Country 'Tis of Thee"—the tune, of course, was plagiarized from "God Save the King," which HPL never tired of reminding him. Once at a party in the Village, Howard remarked: "Mortonius' grandfather wrote 'My County 'Tis of Thee' and Belknapius' grandfather put up the Statue of Liberty." The news was greeted with total disbelief, which was readily understandable.

I was perhaps the most reckless of all the Kalem Club members in one respect. "Foolhardy" would be just as applicable an adjective. I became a free-lance writer at an early age and have remained one ever since, apart from a few years of continuous employment as an associate editor of three all-fiction magazines which did not keep me bent over a desk at an office, since I took all of the work home and brought it back again a week or ten days later, fighting off an impulse to engage in a bout of heavy drinking. It is doubtful whether any of the other members would have embarked upon quite so reckless a course from the beginning. Even Arthur Leeds joined a traveling circus as a boy, and did not settle down to free-lancing until he was thirty. (He often discussed those carefree carnival days and even wrote a story, which he was never able to sell, about a grown man who had a fully developed twin of infant size attached to his chest which never grew any larger. Leeds actually knew him quite well, and they often sat up until the small hours discussing serious works of literature. The gentleman in question later became quite famous, and that teratological anomaly was on view for several years at Hubert's Museum on Forty-second Street.)

The old-fashioned term "agnostic" would come closest to defining my general philosophic attitude toward the universe, although I have always felt that every aspect of "reality" is mysterious beyond belief. I seem to recall that Mark Twain had much the same feeling at times—"Dream other dreams and better"—which places me in very illustrious company indeed. It has always seemed incredible to me that we should be here at all.

I have no more belief in the "occult" than HPL had, even though I have written magazine articles about the paranormal which may seem to belie that assertion. But it was not my fault that the editor mistook for my own beliefs what I had thought I made plain were simply a number of views held by some of my more credulous friends (a few of them quite well-known in academic and scientific circles), for he added to the byline at the head of my article: "By One of America's Foremost Psychics." I have never had any kind of occult experience, place not the slightest credence in tea leaves or Tarot cards, and I am seizing the opportunity which a volume of this nature provides to repair whatever damage that article may have done to my integrity. In setting the record straight, however, there is no reason for me not to add that I believe very firmly in the reality of extrasensory perception and that there may well be certain occurrences that are totally baffling when viewed in the light of what present-day laboratory science has revealed about the nature of reality. Such revelations—and there is nothing wrong with them—are far too incomplete and subject to further experimental modifications to justify dismissing entirely what is generally thought of as the paranormal.

There has been a tremendous resurgence of interest in the past three or four years in what the popular mind has a tendency to term "the occult," and very little discrimination has been shown in drawing distinctions between different types of inexplicable phenomena. In writing for a popular audience in this field as I have occasionally done, I sometimes have not taken sufficient care to be wholly discriminating. This has not been to my credit, for in no field is the drawing of fine distinctions quite so important. Having purged myself, I hope, of past sins in that respect by this public confession, the inclusion here of a few more words concerning what I actually *do* believe becomes necessary.

One's views about almost everything are likely to change, often drastically, across the years. I am filled with both sadness and wry amusement when I recall some of the things I wrote to HPL before 1937. At one point covering a period of several years, I came close to becoming a convert to a ritualistic Catholic mysticism, perhaps because I have always been in rebellion against what I felt was the beauty-ignoring aspect of Protestantism, even when it repudiated every kind of Bible Belt fundamentalism.

Despite his atheism, HPL had great admiration for the liberal Protestant tradition, as he made plain in one of his middle-period letters to me. It is included in the third volume of Arkham House correspondence and was just about the longest letter he ever wrote to anyone. What he failed to realize was that even at that period I had no real intention of becoming a Trappist monk, and it was only the aesthetic-aspects of Roman or Anglo-Catholicism that had made me just a bit less of an agnostic than I had been earlier. Basically, I would never have been able to live for long with any kind of theological orthodoxy, but in challenging some of his most firmly held beliefs, I derived a certain pleasure in playing the part of a Devil's advocate. His ingrained puritanism seemed to me anti-cultural (and there can be no question that puritanism *is* and always has been anti-cultural), and in defending the artist against even the most liberal kind of Protestantism, I cited as ammunition passages from Arthur Symons, Frank Harris, H. L. Mencken (whom he greatly admired), and even Belloc and Chesterton, strange bedfellows indeed. But what these writers did have in common was their abhorrence of the historic blight of Calvinism and its founder, who I have always felt would have been quite capable of burning Shelley at the stake.

My views today have undergone so great a change that while I still feel the same way about puritanism, I find myself more in agreement with HPL's scientific materialism than otherwise, although that agreement is very far from total. But I think the change would have pleased him.

The God beyond God speculations of Paul Tillich—who was, alas, a Protestant theologian—a God who is in many ways opposed to the God of religious orthodoxy and who transcends Him, has a certain appeal for me in my few odd, semi-mystical moments. There is, I feel, a certain relationship between an unusual kind of mysticism and cool, scientific rationality—Blake has to be called a mystic, but he was also a "child of the Enlightenment," which I have not yet worked out to my satisfaction. Perhaps if I live long enough...

The views set forth in the recently published symposium by Alister Hardy, Robert Harvie, and Arthur Koestler, (Alister Hardy, Robert Harvie, and Arthur Koestler, *The Challenge of Chance* [New York: Random House, 1974].) I find totally fascinating, for experiments in the domain of the paranormal conducted on so high a level are rare and few between. They strongly suggest that the portals of the unknown open far wider at times than is commonly believed, and I take such views with the utmost seriousness.

CHAPTER SIX

I can state categorically from my personal knowledge that New York remained a kind of Dunsanian wonder city in Howard's eyes for at least six months, and the disillusionment which occurred later took place so gradually that it did not become oppressive for at least a year.

There was one thing that he never discussed with me—the exact state of his finances. I only knew that he had a small inherited income which was not large enough to warrant extravagance of any kind. It was not even sufficient to enable him to feel justified in turning an indifferent ear to Sonia's constant insistence that if he failed to secure a salaried position within a matter of months, he would be forced to draw on his resources.

Some men might have been tempted to diminish more of their resources than he did in the overly optimistic period that often follows a daring venture into matrimony. But Howard was exceptionally frugal and responsible, even for a New Englander, and if just the thought of job-seeking filled him with misgivings, Sonia's concern made him realize that no delay would be permissible. He became so convinced of this, in fact, that I doubt if anyone ever exposed himself to a more agonizing ordeal, over a period of at least a year, with more persistence and courage.

But it simply did not work out. He was about as remote from the business world of the early 1920s as an Eskimo would have been arriving in Manhattan with some furs strapped to his back and a map of the financial district which someone had given him crumpled between his fingers. He appealed directly to a number of personnel-department directors in the worst of all possible ways. He wrote them long letters, assuring them that he would never allow his genteel New England heritage to interfere with whatever task he might be called upon to perform, provided it was in no way demeaning. He would be quite content with a humble position, and his total lack of experience would naturally preclude one that required a previous business background. He furthermore could type—if slowly—and could answer letters in a simple, direct way, without the slightest trace of literary irrelevance. (Belied, of course, by the very letter which conveyed that information.)

As specimens of employment-seeking correspondence, few letters could have been more incredibly off-target. But surprisingly enough, he received at least four sympathetic replies. Nothing ever came of them, but one was wholly gracious and admirable, a true gentleman's reply on much the same literary level. It would have been difficult for anyone not to be a *little* impressed, no matter how astonished, by a lengthy Lovecraftian epistle.

Sonia once endeavored—and almost succeeded—in securing him a publishing house position. But his total lack of previous office experience, even as a "weeding out" manuscript reader stuck away in some inconspicuous cubicle (a position more readily procurable then, as now, by young ladies fresh out of Vassar), made the firm hesitate at first and then turn thumbs down.

It was outrageous of course and wholly unjustified, for with his literary knowledge, discernment, and ghost-writing experience, Howard would have made an excellent editor, even on the executive level. It gave me a great deal of pleasure to sit quietly listening to him rake most major publishers over the coals in that respect. He did so with a rare kind of detachment, because personal disappointments never enraged or embittered him—only the idiocy and injustice of such policies as they affected two or three of his correspondents, one of whom was a firmly established writer who would have welcomed, between books, the kind of employment that involved no more than a conscientious appraisal of a firm's "slush pile" manuscripts. Who could have been better at that than Howard?

One morning, when a particularly semi-illiterate letter from an advertising concern arrived in the mails, he phoned me in what paradoxically seemed the best of spirits to suggest a visit to the Metropolitan Museum of Art.

"I've decided to get away for a few hours from all of this commercial preposterousness," he said. "If you've the afternoon free I'll meet you in front of the museum at two-thirty. I've got to see those Egyptian exhibits you've been telling me about."

"Two-thirty? Are you sure you can get there as early as that?"

It was not a question I would have asked if he had not been nearly an hour late on two occasions in just the previous fortnight.

"I've a very strong reason for believing so," he said. "Three months in New York and the old gentleman hasn't brushed a single grain of mummy dust off that gray suit that I feel could stand just a little more wear before I follow Sonia's advice and discard it. No one in the Valley of Kings will notice or care how often it has been mended. And this is the first time I've put off anything as important as a visit to the Metropolitan for more than a few days. I can't understand how it could have happened. Three months—my god."

"I'm not sure about the suit," I told him. "If the Pharaohs weren't fashion-conscious why did they insist on being buried with so much pomp?"

I am quite certain I did not actually use the term "fashion conscious" or "style-conscious" because it was not, to the best of my recollection, an expression often heard at that time. But I said something of the sort and added, "It won't matter if you're just a little late. The museum doesn't close before five."

When I returned the receiver to its hook I glanced at the clock and saw that it was one-thirty. I would have to hurry to be at the museum by the specified time, and if Howard surprised me by arriving promptly, I knew he would regard my lateness as a most gratifying occurrence. I had no intention of supplying such a sop to his conscience if I could help it, for he would have continued to use it as an excuse for his own lateness on all subsequent occasions. Scrupulous clockwatching has never seemed too important to me, but there are pretenses which are dangerous to abandon.

I arrived ten minutes late. But there was no sign of him anywhere, and I was just about to go into the museum when I saw him approaching at least three blocks away on the near side of the street. There could be no mistaking Howard's *swift*, slightly jogging walk. He held himself very straight when in motion, with the slight slouch which characterized him in repose conspicuous by its absence. The intervening blocks contained only a few pedestrians, but if the blocks had been crowded with people I would have singled him out instantly, despite his geographical remoteness.

His habit of walking very swiftly without paying much attention to his surroundings often caused him to go plunging across intersections against a red light, at so great a risk to life and limb that his survival in New York for a two year period verged on the miraculous. In Providence the traffic was fortunately less heavy, and his avoidance of accidents until the age of thirty-two was considerably less a miracle.

When he ascended the high stone steps to where I was standing, I was a little surprised, for an instant, that he did not appear to be even slightly out of breath from hurrying.

Then I remembered that he never really hurried. He had simply been striding along at his usual brisk gait.

Howard has been described as "sickly"—a detestable adjective even when applied to invalids, if only because many invalids convey precisely the opposite impression. But it went beyond that with Howard. There was nothing in the least "sickly" about him physically or otherwise, and he was most emphatically not an invalid, if one dismisses his only incapacitating disability—his extreme sensitiveness to below-zero weather. Freezing weather he could not endure and it had a tendency to immobilize him. But otherwise he never seemed to the or become short of breath or experience moments of physical exhaustion. He could slow up slightly on occasion, following some task or journey that was uncongenial to him, but that kind of weariness is nearly universal.

I shall even venture a statement that is certain to be disputed. Whatever Howard may have written in his letters about his semi-invalidism, it was four-fifths a self-delusory distortion. His mother persisted in believing that the "frailness" of health in his youth would prevent him from ever engaging in a strenuously active way in the usual round of adult activities. And unconsciously that seems to have made so profound an impression upon him that he apparently half-believed it. But in the hundreds of letters I exchanged with him, he very seldom referred to himself as even a semi-invalid. Occasionally he did, of course, but it was more the recluse aspect of his daily existence in Providence that he dwelt upon, perhaps knowing that the instant I met him in person that particular departure from reality would go flying out the window.

It was not a particularly crowded day at the Metropolitan Museum. Only a few people were passing in and out, and there was no waiting in line at the turnstiles. (I cannot recall whether there *was* a turnstile just inside the entrance. Certainly no admission desk, for in the 1920s no admission was ever charged for viewing the splendors of the ancient world in the middle of Manhattan. The directors at that period seemed to feel that such a desperately needed change of perspective should be available to all, totally apart from their financial status.)

The Egyptian exhibit was to the right of the entrance on the main floor, and we were standing by a glass-encased mummy imprisoned in its ancient wrappings before we had exchanged more than twenty words of greeting. But from that moment on, Howard became astoundingly eloquent. His erudition in the realm of Egyptology surprised me a little, because it was so extensive in relation to ancient Rome that it could well have crowded out much of slightly less than major importance in the region of the Nile Valley—such as the approximate birth dates of the pre-Dynastic Pharaohs. But insofar as they have been recorded, he could reel them off without a moment's hesitation.

For the next half hour he conducted me on a guided tour of the exhibits, talking continuously and leaving me slightly stunned and a little afraid that if I interrupted him to ask more than a half-dozen questions I would expose the full extent of my ignorance. And being human, that was something I was reluctant to do.

Then we entered the tomb. It was, and remains, the most marvelous of reconstructions, with chambers of authentic Egyptian antiquity narrowing to a burial chamber walled with a kind of faintly perfumed stone slightly pinkish in hue, which I am certain had once known the touch of ancient Egyptian fingers or palms.

It was then that Howard made a mistake later to be regretted. He ran his palm once or twice over the stone, in that most sacrosanct of mortuary chambers.

We visited only the Egyptian exhibits on that particular afternoon, because Howard was to meet Sonia at five and we both were somewhat pressed for time. I left him a block or so from the museum, I seem to recall, and hailed a passing Fifth Avenue bus, knowing that he would soon be on the subway en route to Parkside Avenue and not wishing to delay him by engaging in a discussion which could have gone on for another hour. I knew that it would be on my head if I did, and while Sonia never became angry when one of his friends detained him in this manner, there could be no excuse whatsoever for their failure to realize that Howard could be as irresponsible as a child when he was given the slightest encouragement to engage in a discussion. At such moments time and space ceased to exist for him, and keeping appointments on time became secondary.

The swelling in Howard's hand did not begin until the following morning. Sonia later told me that he was never seriously alarmed about it, even when his hand swelled to twice its normal size. The edema even turned it slightly Egyptian-yellowish in hue, and the puffings did not go down for two or three days. But although he was not greatly worried, his first thought was to phone me about it, and even to phone James Morton and Samuel Loveman who took delight in such occurrences. But he conquered the impulse, and wrote about it instead. It is on record in an early New York letter to Mrs. Gamwell and in another to Alfred Galpin.

The swelling occurred more on the back-of his hand than on his palm. But even his palm swelled sufficiently to make only one inference tenable: he was allergic to the tomb's porous, spice-scented stone wall. Just how much Howard made of this can readily be imagined.

"There are certain people who are *not permitted* to enter ancient burial chambers. The old gentleman is clearly one of them. A kinship was instantly recognized and resented. If I had lingered longer in that tomb, the slumbering malignancy activated by my presence might not have rested content with merely an attack on my hand."

When I saw him the following week there was no stopping him from talking about it, and I decided not even to mention the word "allergy." It would have been a pity to spoil in any way the pleasure which the occurrence had given him. He might at least have conceded that there are different kinds of allergic reactions and that they would not all have to be caused by some chemical substances, but if it pleased him to claim that he was allergic to an invisible presence in the tomb and not to some chemical constituent in the stone itself, well and good. I had seen him rub his palm across the stone, but what of that? There was nothing, surely, to prevent such a presence from incorporating itself into the very texture of the stone as a malign, time-defying guardian of the burial chamber.

Nothing to prevent it but considerations of sobriety and common sense. But if it pleased Howard to brush both aside for a moment and engage in the sort of whimsically humorous pretense that could make his unshakable scientific materialism seem a little less unrelieved by humor, I was entirely in favor of it.

Nothing could quite efface this strain of whimsicality in Howard's nature, not even the shadows which were later to cast so dark a pall on his New York period that if he had not returned to Providence when he did, his sanity might well have been endangered.

We met on an average of three times a week, and it is the amusing incidents that I most like to recall, even though in the interests of biographical accuracy, the tragic deterioration of his marriage must not be slighted. Here are a few of them—the ones that remain so vividly etched on my memory that they almost seem to have taken place as recently as last month.

Howard was fascinated by small articles of stationery—writing pads, rubber bands of assorted sizes, phials of India ink, unusual letterheads, erasers, mechanical pencils, and particularly fountain pens.

He used one pen, chosen with the most painstaking care, until it wore out, and several important factors entered into his purchase of a writing instrument. It had to have just the right kind of ink flow, molding itself to his hand in such a way that he was never conscious of the slightest strain as he filled page after page with his often minute calligraphy. It also had to be a black Waterman; a pen of another color or make would have been unthinkable.

When a pen he had used for several years wore out, the purchase of a new one became an event—lamentable in some respects, but presenting a challenge which I am sure he secretly enjoyed. We were walking northward from Battery Park, where I had met him at noon, stopping occasionally to admire one of the very old houses which still could be found scattered throughout the financial district in the 1920s, when he told me that he intended to purchase a new pen at the first stationery store that had a well-stocked, reliable appearance. He removed the old one from his vest pocket and showed me how worn the point had become. I found myself wondering just how many letters and postcards he had written with it, for it did have a ground-down aspect.

We walked on for three or four blocks, found the kind of store he had in mind, and I accompanied him inside. The clerk who waited on him was amiable and greeted him with a smile when he asked to try out a number of pens.

"The point has to be just right," Howard said. "If it won't put you to too much inconvenience, I'd like to test out at least twenty pens."

The clerk's smile did not vanish when Howard turned to me and said, "I'm afraid this will take some time."

It was just a guess, but I felt somehow that he had made the kind of understatement that would strain the clerk's patience almost beyond endurance.

"We just passed a pipe store," I said. "I'd like to go back and look at the window again. I may just possibly decide to buy a new pipe. I can be back in fifteen or twenty minutes."

"No need to hurry," he said. "I'll probably be here much longer than that."

I was gone for forty-five minutes. It was inexcusable, I suppose, but it was a clear, bright day, a wind with the tang of the sea was blowing in from one of the East River wharves where several four-masted sailing ships were tied, and I decided to go for quite a long walk instead of returning to the pipe shop.

When I got back to the stationery store, there were at least fifty pens lying about on the counter and Howard was still having difficulty in finding one with just the right balance and smoothness of ink flow. The clerk looked a little haggard-eyed but he was still smiling, wanly.

The careful choice of a fountain pen may seem a minor matter and hardly one that merits dwelling on at considerable length. But to me it has always seemed a vitally important key to the basic personality of HPL in more than one respect. He liked small objects of great beauty, symmetrical in design and superbly crafted, and by the same token larger objects that exhibited a similar kind of artistic perfection. And the raven-black Waterman he finally selected was both somber and non-ornate, with not even a small gold band encircling it. That appealed to him in another way and was entirely in harmony with his choice of attire.

His choice of attire conjures up another amusing episode. Howard invariably wore clothes that were conservative in the extreme. He favored dark gray suits, but a dark blue suit would have seemed to him just as appropriate for daily wear; and although to the best of my recollection he never included a black suit in his wardrobe, I am quite certain that he would have worn black with a very comfortable feeling of being appropriately attired. He also favored dark gray or blue socks, without clocks, and plain, dark-colored neckties. Occasionally he wore a polka-dot tie, or one that contained some small, unobtrusive design, but never regimental striped ties, even though they are widely favored by the conservatively attired.

Sonia tried to persuade him to dress a little less conservatively, but her efforts were to no avail. A cravat of bold coloration and striking design—and few artists are capable of resisting an impulse to wear such ties at times—would have seemed to him appropriate only to a bird of paradise flapping its wings in a graveyard. It never occurred to him (and if it did he would have dismissed it as irrelevant) that his attire was in conformity with the wearing apparel of exceptionally conservative bankers and politicians, and was not necessarily closely allied to the New England temperament in its twentieth century incarnation.

About a week after he had purchased the fountain pen, he bought a new hat—probably at Sonia's urging—at a Broadway haberdashery. He seemed in some vague way unhappy about the purchase and suddenly, as we were traveling uptown on the IRT, he took it off and called my attention to it.

"I'm not sure this hat suits an old gentleman," he said. "The clerk was almost insulting when I insisted on trying on more hats than he seemed to want to show me. I came close to losing my temper, but you encounter that kind of discourtesy so often in New York that I'm getting accustomed to it. He wasn't a bad sort, was quite understanding at first, and I probably tried his patience a little. But I simply had to make him understand that I just can't wear *any* hat. The ones in the window wouldn't have suited me at all."

"There's nothing wrong with this one," I said, "from a conservative point of view. It has no flair at all, and little to commend it otherwise. There are many hats I'd much prefer to be found dead wearing. But it's a simple, gray snap-brim. Unless you prefer homburgs—"

"You don't think it's too light in color?"

"I'd say it was medium-gray. What's wrong with that?"

"It seems a little too light in color. And the brim is a little too wide."

"They're wearing wide brims this season," I assured him.

"That's of no consequence," he said. "It has to be suitable for an old gentleman. I may return it."

"It's not worth the bother," I said, feeling a little guilty for having downgraded it so flippantly and without justification; it was a run-of-the-mill hat and looked becoming and inconspicuous enough. "You'll get accustomed to wearing it. Whenever you buy a new suit or hat you wonder if you've made the best possible purchase. I always do. But after a week or so you don't give it a second thought."

"I hope you're right," he said. "It's almost impossible today just to walk into a store and purchase some needed article of wearing apparel that isn't hidden away somewhere. You've got to insist on seeing the things they don't put on display. I could go to Rogers Peat or some other conservative establishment, but their prices are prohibitive."

His misgivings on that occasion were not inconsistent with his refusal to be unprotesting when confronted by something that went contrary to his right to be himself. But what startled me a great deal was a book-purchasing episode which should have gone contrary to his customary avoidance of extravagance. Seemingly it did not, but I did not discover why until later.

The spending spree—it was certainly that—occurred in Brooklyn. He had phoned me to meet him at one of the two or three oldest bookstores in the borough, taking it for granted that I would be sufficiently interested in watching him pick out a number of new additions to his library to make the trip a rewarding one. To watch anyone purchase new books is always a stimulating experience, and he shrewdly guessed that I would need no great urging to join him at the shop with enough spare bills in my wallet to indulge in a little buying myself, if the titles he selected aroused my interest. And I was almost sure that they would. Acts of folly are less likely to be undertaken when there is no goad to set them in motion, which I have always regarded as a saving circumstance. But once the book buying temptation arises, drawing back can be difficult and I know he realized that as well as did I.

Merely by persuading me to join him, Howard was placing me in great jeopardy. It seemed an unworthy subterfuge, but it was difficult to stay angry with him for long. I told myself he probably needed my presence as a restraining influence to keep him from buying more than two or three books.

When I arrived at the bookstore Howard was standing on a movable stepladder at the rear of the shop, removing and examining books from the shelves, putting some of them back and dropping others into the quite large, black-leather shopping bag that he customarily carried even at that early date. (It resembled the large paper bags that are popular with supermarket shoppers, and it accompanied him on all of his later travels in lieu of a briefcase, usually supplemented by a small suitcase when his trips were extensive. Whether it remained the same bag four or five years later, I cannot be certain. It always remained shiny and unworn-looking.)

The instant he saw me, he descended quickly from the stepladder and removed about three books from the bag, stacking them with a pile of four or five previously selected volumes on the book dealer's desk. I then noticed some of the titles: *The Hill of Dreams* by Arthur Machen, *Plays of Near and Far* by Lord Dunsany, and a number of other volumes on colonial America.

"You're just in time to help the old gentleman out," he said. "Your sharp, youthful eyes will keep me from missing something that may be so hidden away and covered with dust I'll overlook it—something I may really want."

"But I don't know what you really want," I said. "You seem to have been ransacking the entire shop."

"There's another ladder right over there," he said, gesturing into the shadows. "Just climb up and look around. If you find anything you feel I should buy, take it down and show it to me."

"How many books do you intend to buy?" I asked.

"Not so many. But I've just started. I will make at least a few more purchases."

I had a vision of Howard leaving the shop with so many books I would have to help him carry them. The proprietor meanwhile emerged from an alcove near the front of the store and seemed pleased by the number of books which Howard had set aside. Toward the end of his foraging, Howard ripped down several volumes and added them to his pile so swiftly that I found myself wondering if he had done justice to whatever interest they had for him. He was up and down the ladder a half-dozen times. I selected one book, and he was so pleased with the title that he did not even open it, but simply nodded and placed it with the others.

Then he spoke with the book dealer for a moment, signed a slip of paper, and bid the man goodbye.

"He'll deliver them tomorrow, in his car," he said as soon as we were outside the store.

"Do you always buy books on impulse that way?" I asked. "I always thought you were very deliberate about spending a fairly large sum of money. The whole transaction would have taken me three times as long. I'd have weighed the cost of each book, and proceeded slowly and with considerable hesitation."

"That's a foolish way of making a purchase," he said. "It doesn't take me long to make up my mind about what I want and what I don't want. You gain nothing by being indecisive."

I did not find out until later—for some reason he had been reluctant to tell me—that he had a bookseller's credit slip for sixty dollars, given to him by J. C. Henneberger, the founder of *Weird Tales*, in lieu of cash payment just before Farnsworth Wright had assumed the editorship of the magazine and story sales on a cash basis had come to an abrupt halt. I have never had any doubt that someone had given Henneberger the credit slip and, being in Chicago, he could not have readily availed himself of a pleasure he had passed along to Howard, without giving much thought to the money he might have saved had he purchased the story for cash.

These incidents have been grouped together because I feel they shed a revealing light on Howard's refusal to take himself with the kind of funereal solemnity that one too often associates with a withdrawn and lonely writer of genius who is so absorbed with the darker aspects of reality that he has no time to devote to those amusingly trivial concerns and inconsistencies that go with a total absence of stuffiness.

Howard never had to worry about his self-image because he wore no mask. His behavior was at all times so natural and spontaneous that he never had to maintain a pose unless it amused him to do so. He often took great delight in insisting that he was "a loyal subject of his Britannic Majesty," "an old gentleman from Providence-Plantations," "an ancient Roman with little patience for the fopperies of the decadent Greeks," "a blunt, rustic, and not very intellectual man of simple tastes" who admired the Old Farmer's Almanac much more than he did "those modern scribblers of avant-garde verse," and perhaps as many as a half-dozen other equally archaic and far-fetched personality identifications that he knew very well could not possibly be taken seriously by his friends.

No one who knew him as well as I did could possibly have been deceived in that respect. He was himself to the core, and that self was so extraordinary that I am quite certain his like will never be seen again. The adoption of a pose—or poses—is so universal a human tendency that one can be sure that it has been resorted to by everyone many times during his life. It is more frequent and compulsive in children than in adults, but it is often compulsive enough in the overwhelming majority of adults.

And it is no crime—without the occasional wearing of masks no one could survive for long. But there are also many different kinds of masks, and when I said that Howard wore *no mask* I simply meant that in his actual personality, he was wholly himself to an extent, perhaps, that one would not be likely to encounter in more than one individual out of a thousand. Basically, he never pretended to be different from the kind of person he was. He knew that all of his "poses," if one *must* employ that term, would be seen through quickly enough and would not be mistaken for any kind of serious pretense.

But one reservation must be made here, and it does not refute what has just been stated. His *eighteenth century* enthusiasms were not a pretense. With some they could well have seemed like a mask-wearing deception, but not with Howard. To visualize him as wearing a periwig and smallclothes never required the slightest imaginative effort on my part. If I could have traveled back in time and met an eighteenth century gentleman of English birth who announced himself as HPL, I would not have questioned his veracity for an instant. A cultivated gentleman of that period with Howard's imaginative gifts would have been entirely in harmony with everything that has been written about the eighteenth century at its most admirable. Moreover, he would have been incapable of deceiving me as to his identity in an age remote from ours. He would have worn no mask, even as an historical simulacrum of his twentieth century self.

CHAPTER SEVEN

I have often wondered what Howard would have thought of life in the United States during the 1970s, since many things were totally different in 1930. It has been said that if one could return after an interval of forty years, or even a century, the changes would seem less startling than the number of things which had remained comparatively unchanged. I have always been doubtful of that, but there is a certain truth in it. The ordinary concerns of daily living would not have changed, but many important things do change; and only when one has remained alive and grown accustomed to the changes gradually, year after year, do they fail to seem particularly startling or different in any great measure.

But there are certainly at least four or five major changes which would have seemed unbelievable to Howard, or left him a little stunned, even if he to some extent could have anticipated them in an imaginative way. The outcome of World War II, with its Nazi concentration camp horrors, would have been one; and the atomic bomb, with all the implications which nuclear fission has left in its wake, would have been another. Few science fiction and fantasy writers failed to anticipate the Bomb at least a decade in advance, but the reality was still rather staggering. And the launching of the first earth satellite, the moon landing, the Cold War, the sexual revolution, the supremacy of television over every other form of entertainment, the motorization of America to an extent undreamed of when Howard was alive—yes, I think his startlement would have been profound.

Some of his attitudes would have been impossible to maintain, and I can picture him abandoning them with more grace and calm acceptance than otherwise. He was open-minded and receptive to change to a greater extent than all his letters might lead one to believe. I doubt if he would have been any more intolerant of the hippies and their extremes of attire and deportment than he was of the Village bohemians of forty years ago. He was not at all seriously antagonistic to the Village rebels of that period. His adherence to more traditional patterns of behavior made him shake his head in disapproval, but he had a great liking for not a few Village artists and writers, and was perfectly at ease in their company.

I was considerably more in accord with the spirit that prevailed at Village parties, but only because I have never found myself disagreeing in any way with the basic assumptions of the rebel artist about a value system that has been grotesquely and outrageously indifferent, in instances too numerous to cite, to the supreme importance of "the music makers and dreamers of dreams."

But speculations of this nature serve no very meaningful or consistent purpose when one's primary object is to depict, through the prism of personal recollections, the kind of person Howard was when he walked the earth. That last phrase may seem a bit grandiloquent, but it is peculiarly relevant notwithstanding, for walking the earth was far from his only preoccupation during the forty-seven years of his life—Howard was a star-treader as well.

There is no better way of providing a rounded portrait of Howard as he was than to dwell for a moment on his reading; on all the books that were influential in providing him with the bedrock of information that must be acquired in the course of the years if a man is not to remain wholly a child.

There was a quite extensive and diversified library in the large, rambling old house on Angell Street where Howard spent his early years. In addition to the eighteenth century and the smaller number of Victorian English volumes which the Phillips library contained, there were not a few about the deathless gods of Greece and Rome. In his classical reading, Howard preferred the Roman gods to the Greek ones, but in a moment of absolute candor he once confided to me that he felt the Romans could have done better than merely to have borrowed their gods from the Greeks and Latinized their names.

Mythology, as he never became tired of stressing, had exerted a most profound influence upon him as a child and had found in him the kind of reader responsiveness that is becoming increasingly rare in the modern world. To Howard the ancient world was always as real as the other side of a looking glass that held no dangerous shapes of any kind. He could enter it without fear, even as a very young child, because there were no monstrous gorgons or other mythological entities that could threaten him in any physical way. Beyond that looking glass there was only a fantasy world supreme, and when he became a part of it, he wore the sort of imaginative shield which only a young scientific materialist might depend upon at all times. For Howard believed in nothing that observation had failed to confirm.

There can be no doubt that all of Howard's writing in later years was influenced by his early familiarity with the timeless tales of classical antiquity in which gods and human heroes often battled for supremacy in a contest in which such self-assertiveness on the part of mortals had of necessity to be veiled by a pretense of obedience. There was something in Howard's nature which makes me think that while he saw no hope at all for mankind when "Great Cthulhu and all the other Old Ones awoke from their age-long slumber," he would himself have done battle until no longer capable of drawing breath. He is the only individual in all of his stories—and he appears in the thinnest of disguises in many of them—who would have belied the character traits that he was depicted as possessing. The "Old Gentleman from Rhode-Island and Providence-Plantations" would have hurled thunderbolts of defiance to the end, firmly standing his ground. To have fled, shrieking and cringing down the corridors of time, only to have been overtaken in the end, would not have been in accord with the behavior standards of an "aging" New England gentleman.

Howard, in truth, possessed no actual fear of the unknown at any time in his life. He did not feel that there was anything to justify such fear when death, in his eyes, was only a long forgetting and more to be welcomed than otherwise.

Howard never quite shared the childlike wonder and wild surmise in the presence of the ancient gods and human heroes that Samuel Loveman did, simply because even as a very young child he was capable of imagining more terrible entities buried in the depths of the sea and beyond the universe of stars. But the ancient tales fascinated him in many other ways. This is evident in the frequent references, in many of the stories written during his Dunsanian period, to a mythology that was partly Dunsanian and partly Greco-Roman. In Lord Dunsany's own mythos, the gods were largely his own, but like HPL, he did borrow quite extensively from classical mythology.

It is perhaps worth noting here that Dunsany was also profoundly influenced by the King James Bible, particularly in the cadenced simplicity and splendor of his best writing. Was Howard? I have often asked myself that question, because in all of his letters or conversations, he never once said that he had been influenced directly by the King James version or any other Biblical translation.

I do not know why I never asked him. Perhaps I may have taken for granted either one of two things: One—the Bible was at such variance with Howard's cosmological conception of a vast, inscrutable universe, that he could not have allowed it to intrude, even on a stylistic level, into any of his writings. (It was permissible for that universe to harbor Great Old Ones of a hoary, Cthulhuian antiquity, but not the Song of Songs nor the wholly human, very Freudian sex life of King Solomon.) Two—there conceivably may have been no King James version of the Bible in his grandfather's library, and having failed to be influenced by the rhythmic splendor of that edition in his most impressionable years, it was only much later in his Dunsanian period that a Biblical cadence occasionally crept into his own writing. In general, that particular kind of prose was not conspicuous in his stories, even in the early ones. His style was quite different from Dunsany's in many ways, even in that somewhat imitative period, and the wholly original, much greater Mythos tales were certainly not stylistically Biblical.

There can be no doubt that Howard was familiar with the Bible, for he did mention, in both his letters to me and to others, that his attitude toward it was no different from the total non-orthodoxy of Thomas Huxley, and I am certain that by a fairly early age he could have quoted Huxley at some length. But it still remains possible that there was no King James Bible in his grandfather's library to enable him to absorb its stylistic splendors, almost by osmosis, as so many other authors in embryo have done.

It is in the field of classical studies that the osmosis possibility must be accorded some weight. His ability as a child to reel off the names of a thousand and one classical deities, from the stately denizens of Mount Olympus to the evanescent spirits of wood and grove, verged upon the miraculous.

He could have told you that Melpomene was the muse of tragedy, Thalia of comedy, and, particularly of importance to himself some ten or twelve years later, that Urania was the muse of astronomy. He could have drawn a sharp distinction between the activities of two somewhat similar gods—Themis the god of Divine Justice and Dike of Human Justice, who sit enthroned on opposite sides of Zeus. And he knew as well what must be whispered at the shrine of Apollo if one requires assistance from the Lord of the Silver Bow.

Whether or not he would have agreed at the age of six with the often quoted line: "All-conquering are the shafts made from the Vine," is a moot question. But it is doubtful whether total abstinence from alcohol would have seemed important to him as a child! Otherwise nothing in Greek or Roman mythology would have seemed unimportant to him as a necessary kind of knowledge for a truly cultivated person. Pride in erudition was one aspect of the maturity that he seems to have felt must be acquired as swiftly as possible, to avoid the need of constant self-reproach.

When I first began to correspond with HPL, his literary tastes were wide and varied, although he still read Dr. Johnson and Alexander Pope with undiminished admiration. But the work of every established contemporary fiction writer of the early 1920s he could discuss at considerable length and with a perceptiveness that removed all doubt as to the modernity of his knowledge in that one area. It would be impossible to do full justice to the range of his reading as an adult in fiction alone, and the need for condensation here enables me to succumb to a whim I have always felt would be highly amusing—the making of a list of HPL's "favorite" writers, all apart from the time of their arrival in the literary firmament, juxtaposing recently departed authors with long-buried ones in a nonsequential fashion.

The list would read as follows: Lord Dunsany, Dr. Johnson, Kipling (his early macabre tales), Algernon Blackwood (*The Willows*), Pope, Arthur Machen (*The Great God Pan, The Hill of Dreams, The White People*), Oliver Wendell Holmes (*Elsie Venner*), Hawthorne (*The Marble Faun, The House of the Seven Gables*), William McFee (*Casuals of the Sea*), Edgar Allan Poe (complete and unabridged, many times revisited), Samuel Butler (*The Way of All Flesh*, with its devastating exposure of Victorian hypocrisy), Robert W. Chambers (*The King in Yellow*), M. P. Shiel (*The House of Sounds*), Ambrose Bierce (*Can Such Things Be?*), Walter de la Mare (the macabre short stories), Defoe (whom he liked, including *Moll Flanders*, better than Fielding or Smollett), Joseph Hergesheimer (*Java Head*), Charles Brockden Brown (*Wieland*), William Hope

Hodgson (*The House on the Borderland*), J. Sheridan Le Fanu (*The Legend of the Glaive*), M. R. James (a dozen of perhaps the greatest purely ghostly tales ever written).

Of course I have omitted a few authors who were numbered among HPL's prime favorites; no list of this nature could ever be complete.

Another list, including all of the writers he had read who could not have been numbered among his *prime* favorites, and including a few whom he actively disliked, might be as follows: Theodore Dreiser, Sinclair Lewis, Dryden, Walt Whitman, Dostoevsky, Sherwood Anderson, Thomas Hardy, Shaw, Galsworthy, Conrad, Marlowe, Thoreau, Henry James, Edith Wharton, H. G. Wells, Voltaire, Balzac, Jonathan Swift, and on and on, in the mixed-up sequence that still seems to me amusing somehow, although it makes no real sense.

Dickens may well have been a greater novelist than Tolstoy or Dostoevsky, but HPL hated Victorian sentimentality so profoundly that, to be absolutely safe, I have omitted him from the second list. I must also add parenthetically that many of the writers I have excluded from the first list he recognized as very great, and he could be just as imaginatively and emotionally stirred by many passages in their books as by the much smaller number of very special volumes that he treasured as a writer of supernatural horror stories, since he found in them the darkly evocative moods that paralleled his own nightside explorations.

A great many fiction writers devote more reading hours to novels and poetry than to works of philosophy, science, or a program of reading so generalized that it embraces ten, fifty, or even a hundred branches of knowledge. Although Howard's reading did not exactly fall within the extreme limits of the third category, it was certainly the opposite of restricted. His interest in all of the natural sciences remained on the same level of intensity as his antiquarian interests from his early years onward. And that level could hardly have been higher.

I have often thought that the Roman poet-philosopher Lucretius best exemplified the approach to science that was most characteristic of Howard. Like every other ancient world thinker, Lucretius was encapsulated within the limited framework of knowledge available to him at the time. Yet within that framework he actually worked out a speculative approach to man's origin and destiny that was not very different from Darwin's theory of natural selection.

Like Lucretius, HPL maintained a critically rational approach to the observable aspects of reality. He thought that only minds capable of discarding every instilled traditional belief concerning man's place in the universe were worthy of respect as investigators of the unknown. All such investigations, he realized, encountered pitfalls. But with patient persistence many of the pitfalls could be avoided, and there were not a few contemporary men of science who were very good in this regard.

"Contemporary" for Howard, of course, spanned the period from about 1915 to 1937, and in those years Einstein's fame was increasing while Eddington and Jeans were only slightly less famous, although Eddington forfeited a little of Howard's admiration because of his slightly mystical bias. There was not a page of Jeans that Howard failed to read, and if Hoyle had also been a contemporary, I know he would have been even more fascinated by what this author believes about a universe which appears to be in a constant state of renewal, creating vast new galaxies out of hydrogen gas.

To Howard the modern titan was Einstein (not Freud), and the Victorian counterpart, Darwin. He probably would have conceded, if pressed, that Marx was another titan, but he was never a Marxist, even though in his last few years he became converted, first to a New Deal liberalism, and finally to a kind of democratic socialism that was closely in accord with the ideology of Norman Thomas or Carl Sandburg. Since he started off as an ultra-conservative in the socio-political domain, a change of that magnitude for him could scarcely have constituted a more dramatic reversal.

Of enormous importance in relation to the direction taken by Howard's writing, was the impression which pictorial art made upon him in an imaginatively stimulating way from his early youth. The influence of painting must undoubtedly be placed in much the same relation to the molding of the Mythos as the influence of books. It was not to the same extent a profoundly germinal influence, but had he lacked all familiarity with the masters of the macabre, the fantastic, and the cosmic in nineteenth and twentieth century pictorial art, his stories would, I am convinced, have failed to attain quite the heights that they did in their evocation of the terrifyingly somber and "night land" grotesque. They might, it is true, still have possessed qualities which no influence could greatly enhance, such as a feeling for vast, monster-shadowed regions of otherwise empty space beyond the universe of stars. But there would have been fewer sepulchre-inhabiting entities of quite such chilling contours if he had never looked at a painting by Goya or Rops.

Goya was, of course, a realistic painter preoccupied with the horrors of war. But he was a supreme master of the imaginatively macabre as well, and Howard ignored the realism and interpreted the ghastliness in a different way. It was always the skull beneath the flesh that made Goya's vision so unique, and it was not just an ordinary kind of skull even in those simple, "pastoral" scenes of a group of Spanish peasants facing a firing squad with their features convulsed with horror. HPL experienced no difficulty in imagining how the victims of war's brutality might look if the flesh of their faces dissolved, and they returned as "Outsiders" in some ghastly Hispanic crypt, thirsting for the vengeance denied them in life.

Howard did not often discuss the work of the early Dutch and Flemish painters and the kind of surrealistic influence which they have exerted on European painting in general across the centuries. What probably prejudiced him a little against them was the extent to which medieval religious concepts dominated their thinking. But other concepts figured just as prominently, and in an age which was almost incredibly naive and childish in many ways, the dream imagery which they conjured up was so sophisticated in a modern sense that it would have triumphantly confirmed what Jung believed about archetypal images.

But Howard did not quite view the matter that way. The demoniac visions of Hieronymus Bosch *must* have enlarged his understanding of what certain very special tomb-dwellers might be capable, but only after he had transformed them into something rather different from the small, scurrying, sharp-toothed and rodent-like imps that cavort in such a suggestive and hideous way in these paintings. Men and women with the heads of animals, embryonic horrors emerging from eggs, lecherous monsters with forked tails, might well have suggested to Howard some Pickman's Model image in more than one of his macabre stories, but he would have left out the flickering fires arising from potholes in a medieval inferno, and substituted some chill, barren landscape with an aura of cosmic alienage hovering over it. And the monster would also have been considerably different. And yet—I suspect that Howard did borrow at times a dream image or two, enlarged and subtly altered from Bosch or from Pieter Brueghel the Younger or from the German painter and etcher, Lucas Cranach.

In one of his middle-period Providence letters to me, Howard wrote: "The process of delving into the black abyss is to me the keenest form of fascination, and it is my conviction that this process demands the exercise of those parts of the human organism which represent the latest and most complex degree of evolution. I burn, I admire, I respect...and what I crave, admire, and respect is the pure and abstract abyss-plunging which enthralled Anaxagoras, Anaximenes, and Anaximander." (H. P. Lovecraft, *Selected Letters III,* ed by August Derleth and Donald Wandrei [Sauk City: Arkham House, 1971], p. 299.)

He could well, I think, have added "the early Flemish painters," despite their credulous medievalism on a demoniacal level. For they did plumb the black abyss and transfer to canvas the kind of dream imagery that seems always to be accompanied by the beating of gigantic bat wings.

CHAPTER EIGHT

There was another aspect of paintings which evoked for Howard visions of the wholly marvelous and brought him close to the Edge of the World. That Edge, in Lord Dunsany's *The Book of Wonder,* bordered upon "the unreverberate blackness of the abyss," and once one toppled over, he was hurtled onward forever with no echoing sounds to relieve the awfulness of the journey. But before that happened, in the thatched-roofed shadow of some small peasant cottage, with the golden splendors of the Edge, its snow-capped mountains, its lakes and valleys stretching to some wholly enchanted horizon—one became filled with the most glorious kind of adventurous expectancy.

The paintings of Nicholas Roerich—"Old Nick," as Howard always called him—provided precisely this kind of enchantment for Howard on three of his later visits to New York. They were housed in the Riverside Museum, a few blocks from where I resided, and he would stand before each of the paintings for two or three minutes without saying a word. Then he would go into a kind of lyrical ecstasy and pass on to another painting.

"There's something space-and-time dissolving about those distant mountain peaks in the twilight. A rhythm, a kind of cosmic droning, seems to emanate from them. Old Nick hardly ever painted anything else—just distant mountain peaks silhouetted against the sky, and now I can understand why. He knew how to make every slope of the Himalayas magical in a different way, just by resorting to incredible gradations of light and shadow. Every painting is totally different, unique of its kind, and there is nothing even slightly monotonous about them. Yet superficially they are very much alike and that, too, is part of the magic."

In a glass case at the entrance to the exhibit there were several photographs of "Old Nick," depicting a man of advanced years with a slightly oriental cast of features and a small beard. And one very early portrait of the artist in his youth, wearing a flowing tie and looking strikingly Byronic against a background of snow and ice.

And many art exhibition honor ribbons, in pale blue with gold seals attached to them. Testimonial tributes as well, some in Russian, others in English and French.

"I've a feeling, if you asked him, he'd have given up all those honors to be that youth of twenty-two again," I can remember telling Howard.

"I don't think so," Howard said. "The trouble with the young today is their total inability to appreciate the accomplishments of a man of advanced years. Blake was eighty when he painted his crowning achievement, *The Day of Judgment*."

Even though Blake was the opposite of orthodox in any traditional religious sense, it surprised me to hear Howard praise a painting so Biblical in its imagery. I was quite certain he would not have done so under ordinary circumstances, but my implied tribute to youth at the expense of the "aging" had clearly made him feel that he must seize upon the first convincing example that came to mind of how mistaken I was.

He was right, of course, about the achievements of men between sixty and ninety in the realm of the arts. Cervantes was well past sixty when he wrote *Don Quixote,* as was Defoe when he wrote *Robinson Crusoe,* and Shakespeare when he wrote *The Tempest,* which contains passages of poetic splendor equaling, if not surpassing, the earlier plays. A hundred and one other examples could be cited in the literature of the western world. I have always had the feeling that in Chinese literature, for some reason I cannot explain, the writings of ancient sages topped the list.

If pressed, Howard might well have gone further and affirmed that no one could be more ancient than himself, and that he had written at least a few stories which we both agreed were superior to the ones conceived in his Dunsanian period when he had experienced a slight stirring of youthfulness in himself, a resurgence of something that then had come to life. In that earlier period, Dunsany had set him dreaming of the imperishable cities in *The Book of Wonder* which had remained uneroded by anything as inconsequential as the passing of time, while *Idle Days on the Yann* had made him feel neither young nor old, but simply a "dreamer of the spheres, by some strange mischance come hither hurled."

On that particular afternoon, on leaving the museum, we took a thirty block walk along Riverside Drive, and sat down on a bench for perhaps an hour to discuss a number of things—I seem to be quoting from Lewis Carroll here—that were not directly related to art. Since I started this chapter by dwelling upon the influence which certain paintings undoubtedly had on Howard, both in his formative years and later, my recalling some of the matters we discussed may be a little out of place here. But I cannot resist an impulse to do so, for they covered so wide a range and were of such absorbing interest to me, as I am certain they were to him, that they shed a revealing light on how alike we were, in the domain of shared views, and also how different. I was so unlike Howard in many ways that the differences greatly exceeded the similarities. (The same thing could probably be said of any two individuals selected at random, regardless of their race, age, hereditary endowments and environmental conditioning, and no matter how much they had, or failed to have, in common.)

I began that exchange of views by being wholly myself: an extremely self-centered youth who possessed not a few admirable qualities, but who was sadly lacking in realistic understanding of the people, events, and places that encroached upon that self-centeredness. I had read widely, but without much discrimination, was self-indulgent and somewhat lazy, and took short cuts whenever possible to avoid tasks of an uncongenial nature, no matter how important they were when soberly considered in relation to what the future is certain to demand of a mature individual who knows exactly where he is headed and what his chances of survival are in a world where blind chance plays a larger role than individual effort.

"I'm becoming more and more convinced I made a mistake in leaving college and becoming a free-lance writer just on the strength of a few story sales," I told Howard. "Important as writing is, I could have been completely happy if I had a secure position in a field that has always had a tremendous emotional and imaginative appeal for me—that of natural history. I should have secured an MA and applied for a job as assistant curator or something of the sort on the staff of a museum. I could have continued writing in my leisure hours. I could even have gone in for teaching, except that I do not feel I would make a very good teacher. To be a good teacher you have to have the kind of classroom presence that doesn't permit you to be carried away by some particular enthusiasm and talk your head off, at the risk of seeming a little ridiculous."

"As I do at times," Howard said. "I understand exactly what you mean."

"I don't think you do," I said. "You would have made a splendid teacher. You talk in a calm, assured way, no matter how swiftly. And you possess just the right kind of academic dignity."

"An elderly professor in some backwater college—yes, I suppose I could qualify for that kind of teaching post," Howard conceded.

"That isn't what I meant at all," I assured him. "You could talk a full Harvard professor under the table, and do it in such a way that he would look out at you with awe. As for the students—" I became suddenly serious. "Whenever I visit the American Museum, I find myself wishing I could have worked on one of the habitat groups—along with other staff members, wearing a lab smock, picking up some bright-plumaged tropical bird and setting it down again. It would have been the right kind of career for me. I would also have been assured of economic security. But that would have been the smallest part of it."

"You could still do it," Howard said. "You're certainly still young enough to spend five more years in college with no feeling that you're getting on in years."

"It's too late for that now," I said. "I gambled on making a living writing for the magazines and I'll have to go right on turning out stories."

"You've a far better chance than I have of striking the popular fancy. I can only write one kind of story. You can write in several different veins."

"The three stories I sold that were not aimed at *Weird Tales* were pretty terrible," I reminded him. "You said so yourself." (At that time I had sold one adventure story, one historical romance monstrosity, and one haunted house narrative which had appeared in the short-lived MacFadden magazine, *Ghost Stories*.)

"There's something I've never told you," I said, to change the subject. "When I was about thirteen, I was absolutely determined to run away from home and explore the great rain forests of the Amazon. The determination gripped me most strongly when I was roaming the corridors of the American Museum. But I doubt if I would have gotten any further than the Staten Island ferry."

"The yearning for exploration and high adventure in obscure corners of the earth which most boys, if they are at all imaginative, experience between the ages of ten and thirteen, is something I've never experienced myself to quite that extent," Howard conceded. "But I can well understand it, and a very slight difference in my early background might have made me dream of actually running away without saying a word to anyone about it. Naturally I wouldn't have done anything of the sort and neither would you, for you are as attached to your family as I am to mine. I did all of my exploration in the pages of books."

"But some kids have actually done it," I said. "Just packed up and left home, and hitched a ride on a freight train."

"Usually boys from broken families in impoverished circumstances," Howard said. "Very rough-and-tumble types. The very fact that you singled out the Amazon indicates that you didn't have the remotest intention of going through with it. Unless he looked at least five years older, a thirteen year old boy would have no more chance of getting to Brazil on a tramp steamer than a six year old would of getting as far as twenty blocks from his home on the back of an ice wagon."

(There were horse-drawn ice wagons in New York on which children of that age or a little older frequently bummed rides when I was eight, but it surprised me a little that the same opportunity had apparently existed in Providence at an earlier period, and that Howard could refer to horse-drawn vehicles of that nature with such an air of familiarity in the late 1920s when they had become completely obsolete.)

I glanced at Howard and saw that he appeared to be smiling. He could smile quite broadly at times, and this imparted a very animated look to the lower part of his face, even when his eyes were in shadow, as they were now because of the way the overhanging branches above the bench arched down close to his head.

"I don't think you'd make such a good museum staff worker," he said. "You'd roam all over the museum looking at the exhibits. You'd spend at least an hour every day in the Insect Hall alone—I'm sure of it. Tropical butterflies as big as dinner plates with iridescent wings, leaf insects which are miracles of protective mimicry, trap door spiders and tarantulas—live ones, remember, in a big glass case?—and case after case filled with nothing but brightly-carapaced beetles. And the Hall of Marine Invertebrates, with the best sea-shell exhibit in the United States, and the sporting whales and dolphins."

"What in Pegana's name are you getting at?"

"It's the beauty and wonder of natural history that appeals to you, not the dull, routine work that a scientific investigator in any field has to engage in. Do you know how much patient labor a museum worker has to devote just for mounting and classifying a single case of insects? You wouldn't care nearly as much for that part of it. And you'd have to spend nine-tenths of your time doing nothing else."

"Aren't you exaggerating a little?"

"I don't think so. What you lack, Belknapius, is a capacity for rigorous, self-imposed discipline. If a scientific worker in any field doesn't possess that capacity he'd better throw in the towel immediately."

Howard could make use of semi-slang lingo quite effectively when an occasion called for it, including sports column colloquialisms. But this was hardly what nettled me. It was that *he* should have said something like that, in view of the way he felt about retyping a story, even a short one that had been rejected by an editor with a promise of acceptance if he would spend no more than an hour double-spacing it.

I decided to change the subject again.

"There's time enough left to take in that Civil War movie I told you about, unless you'd prefer to sit here talking. I hate to miss it—it won't be on next week."

"I don't think I could sit through it. From what I've heard it's about as historically synthetic as the one I saw last month in Providence that made the War between the States seem like low comedy. You'd hardly expect Grant to conduct himself like General Burgoyne, but I didn't like to see even Grant caricatured by what was done to that picture."

"Besides," he added, "you told me it was playing at the 103rd Street Theatre and that's a long walk back. Why don't we just sit here and talk for a while longer?"

Grant's tomb was up ahead, and I could only hope that there would not be a faint, ghostly stirring inside of it, because of what Howard had said. He had come to Grant's defense, in a way, but I am quite certain that the General could hardly have been pleased by the comparison which HPL had drawn between "Gentleman Johnny" Burgoyne and himself.

Although Howard actually professed to take little interest in the Civil War since it followed by many years the colonial period in which, as a loyal subject of the British crown, he felt more historical kinship, he did have great respect for Grant. Lee may have possessed many qualities which he admired, but Grant impressed him as the blunt, "no nonsense" kind of soldier that a New Englander could understand. For Sherman he had much less respect, for he felt that the March to the Sea had been barbaric in the extreme. Although I had no inclination to dispute that, I found it a little difficult at times to restrain myself from reminding him that the behavior of certain British generals had been just as barbaric on occasion and that if he had been trapped inside a burning Washington in the War of 1812, he would not have enjoyed it at all. He probably would have countered by pointing out that great care had been taken to remove all civilians from the city in advance, but that would not have been true.

We were still sitting on the bench when a sunset glow crept over the Palisades and the conversation had virtually ended. But there was one more thing I wanted to discuss with him and felt that it would take no more than five or six minutes before there was any urgent need to get up and retrace our steps along the Drive. He was to be our guest at dinner on that particular evening, but we still had an hour or so to spare.

"I was quite serious when I spoke about securing a museum job," I said. "But your whole attitude in regard to what you'd most like to do is different from mine. You accept all disappointments and frustrations without becoming emotionally excited or angry or embittered, or even just slightly depressed. How can you be so stoical or fatalistic—I don't care what term you use. Doesn't it get to you in a very serious, vital way? Don't you ever consider how different everything would be if you had absolute economic security or you sold every story you submitted to a magazine and didn't have to do so much tedious revisory work? Or you could travel as much as you pleased, without giving a thought to expenses? Or live in some rambling old house in Providence just like the one on Angell Street which you seem almost to be living in still at times, from the way you talk about it? What if you could buy back the Phillips residence, and had enough left over to free you of all strain for the next forty years?"

"I might not be any happier if I could do all of those things," he said. "Something else could come along that would make all of the pleasure meaningless. If I lost both of my aunts, for instance. What could be worse than that for an old gentleman who has no other close family ties left that can provide a feeling of being close to the past and every treasured memory of childhood? It may happen soon enough, but until it does why should I torment myself, and become angry and embittered, as you phrase it, just because there are some other things I would very much like to have? There is no certainty that you will long possess anything—no assurance of any kind of permanence as far as possessions are concerned. And that applies just as much to travel and financial security. You may travel for one year and be afflicted with some lingering illness that will never permit you to do so again. Being confined to Providence for the next twenty years would not be much of a hardship for me, but the illness would make the other things you mention of far less value. At best, they would lose two-thirds of their value."

There was very little that I could say in rebuttal. When a point of view is presented with that kind of eloquence and persuasiveness, it is best to fall silent. I had no intention of nodding in agreement, for I was not in accord with much of what he had said. But he deserved the tribute of silence, and after we arose from the bench we walked two full blocks before I spoke again.

On the long return journey, Howard began talking about my poetry, as he often did. My second volume of verse, *The Goblin Tower*, was several years in the future. It would not appear until Howard visited Robert H. Barlow in Florida where they put it together as a surprise and sent me five unbound copies, and one handsomely bound in leather accompanied by a brief note which read: "Happy birthday! Hope you approve of the selections. We didn't have too many poems to choose from."

(That Florida visit is on record in an early Arkham House book. Barlow's tragic death by his own hand in Mexico would have come as a very great shock to Howard, as it did to me. I met him only once, when he stayed for a day and a half at a New York hotel before boarding a train for Providence. But I had previously exchanged eight or ten letters with him. He was seventeen at the time—nineteen when Howard died. He was a gifted poet, shy and sensitive and withdrawn, and what I remember most about that brief visit was the photograph he showed me of Jules Verne on his bier, which he had gone to the length of having reproduced from a negative at either the Forty-second Street Library or the New York Historical Society. He later became so famous an archeologist in the pre-Columbian field that his suicide was followed by a two column obituary in the *New York Times.)*

The poems that Howard liked best in my first volume of verse, *A Man from Genoa (*Frank Belknap Long, *A Man from Genoa, and Other Poems* [Athol, Massachusetts: W. P. Cook, 1926].)*,* were the title poem itself, *The Prophet, On Reading Arthur Machen, The Marriage of Sir John de Mandeville,* and *Manhattan Skyline.* But just then, the leafy boughs of one particular tree on the far side of the Drive seemed for a moment to assume the shape of a gibbet when stirred by the wind, and I thus was prompted to recite one of the other works from this collection. We were, after all, discussing the volume as a whole, and there was nothing unusual about singling out one poem to intone aloud that I particularly wished to call his attention to, since he had omitted it from his list of preferred poems.

"I've always rather like this one," I said, and recited all ten of the lines.

TWO STANZAS FOR MASTER FRANCOIS VILLON

A man there was who had no hair at all
To warm a graceless and a chastened head;
For thirty winters he had know the fall
Of leaves upon the stones his feet would tread
Until his hopes and all his fears were dead.
A man there was who had no teeth nor hair,
And Justice stalked him till he nimbly fled;
But though his cronies walked upon the air,
And though the Devil mapped the life he led,
He someone glittered—and his songs are read.

"Are you sure Villon had no hair or teeth left when he was thirty?" Howard asked. "It seems incredible. You make him seem like the old gentleman—and even I haven't reached quite that stage of decrepitude."

"I read that somewhere," I told him. "Maybe it was in Robert Louis Stevenson. No hair at all—"

"How would Stevenson know? To confirm it you'd have to travel back to the fifteenth century and secure an autopsy report from the barber-surgeon who dissected him vein by vein, as they did in those days when a corpse was delivered into the hands of medical school instructors to enlarge what little they knew about human anatomy. No doubt he was picked up in the last stages of alcoholic poisoning in some cobblestoned alleyway in a Paris that was just as decadent as it has become today. A graceless wight. I like your Sir John de Mandeville much better."

And he quoted the opening stanzas of

THE MARRIAGE OF SIR JOHN DE MANDEVILLE

Because the King of Travelers
Had sworn that he would wive
The golden roofs were thronged with heads
Of every lad alive.
A thousand shawms were lightly blown,
A thousand drums were beat;
And young Sir John de Mandeville
Came riding down the street.
He was a wiry knight and brave,
A foolish knight and wise;
And he had flaming caravans
And suns within his eyes.

This is the only time I have taken a very slight liberty with an actual occurrence. It did not happen in quite so well synchronized a way. Howard may even have quoted the de Mandeville poem first, and that gibbet I thought I saw on the far side of the Drive may have been dredged from my unconscious for the first time just a minute or two ago, to supply a heightened dramatic touch to my memory of what was said. But in a way—it has very much the ring of truth, at least for me.

CHAPTER NINE

A month or so before Howard's marriage, J. C. Henneberger, the founder and owner of *Weird Tales,* decided to publish in a forthcoming issue a long novelette bearing the name of the famous magician, Harry Houdini, whom he knew quite well. He had a few rough notes which Houdini had sent him, and these he turned over to Howard, suggesting that he undertake the actual writing of the story. Howard saw no reason to ignore an opportunity to assume a ghost-writing task which he felt would prove highly congenial, for the story was to be titled *Imprisoned with the Pharaohs* and would deal with the almost entirely imaginary adventures of Houdini himself amidst Egyptian horrors which Howard was quite certain he could render convincingly.

The story of what happened to the original manuscript—how it had been lost in the station at Providence, and then laboriously reconstructed on a borrowed hotel typewriter while Howard was in Philadelphia on his honeymoon excursion—is on record elsewhere, both in Sonia's own words and in a reference in one of his letters to Mrs. Clark; so I shall not dwell upon it here. He never once discussed it with me and I can shed no additional light, although several slightly different versions of it filtered through to me later.

I have no reason to question the authenticity of Sonia's account.

Howard did discuss with me his meeting with Houdini, and this is a matter of singular interest simply because Houdini remains, despite the years which have passed since his death, almost as unforgettable a figure in the popular mind as he was when Howard met him in the early 1920s. Even those who are far too young to have seen him perform remember him as a legend, in that strange way that youth has of recalling events that have been witnessed in some other dimension of space and time.

He was undoubtedly the greatest escape artist who ever existed, and his like will probably never be seen again. Ray Bradbury recently described, in a television interview, the thrill which his two daughters experienced when he introduced them to Thurston in a Los Angeles bookstore. But Houdini was an even greater master of illusion, and thrilled millions in a somewhat different way, by seeming to expose himself to the kind of personal danger which it was difficult for any member of an audience not to feel might easily have a fatal outcome.

At Houdini's invitation Howard arrived at the long-vanished New York Hippodrome when he was giving one of his peak performances. An hour or so before the curtain went up, the master magician slipped quietly into the chair adjacent to the one that HPL occupied, introduced himself, and began to converse.

And as he talked, Howard told me the following day, he had the strange illusion, several times repeated, that Houdini was not there at all. Only his voice seemed to come from some region immeasurably remote, and Howard never once glanced sideways to dispel the illusion; to have done so would have gone contrary to the stern attitude he always took about succumbing to any kind of silly credulity that could be dismissed as meaningless if one took the trouble to analyze it. It left enough of an impression on him to make him feel he should at least mention it to someone later. That someone happened to be myself, and of that I was glad, since had it been anyone else I am quite certain that individual would been tactless enough to persist in talking about it at least for a few minutes. Howard would not have wanted that at all; although it was one of those absurdities he was not entirely capable of keeping to himself, he would have had no desire to discuss it at length. To spare him I simply said: "You get that feeling sometimes when you're talking with someone you've met for the first time. If you fail to look at him continuously, I mean. All voices vary in pitch, and a new voice seems to do so more than it ordinarily would if you were familiar with its inflections."

Before the time arrived when Houdini's presence was required backstage, they had discussed a number of things, including the splendid job Howard had done in "revising and expanding" *Imprisoned with the Pharaohs* (not once did Houdini mention ghost-writing), what an exceptionally farsighted businessman Henneberger was, the serious disagreements he had had with Baird, and why it was just possible that a new editor might soon be at the helm of *Weird Tales*.

A short while later Henneberger offered HPL the editorship of

Weird Tales, thus confirming what I have always believed: in some strange way that meeting with Houdini had been just a little more than an ordinary get-together arranged by Henneberger at Houdini's request, ostensibly to permit him to convey in person his appreciation for what Howard had accomplished in adding a few "heightened dramatic touches" to *Imprisoned with the Pharaohs.*

The performance which Howard witnessed that night greatly impressed him. Houdini had appeared on the stage manacled from head to toe, descended into a towering water tank, and emerged five minutes later dripping wet, holding one padlock aloft in his hand as a symbol of triumph.

"He's a strange little man," Howard said, when I asked him what kind of impression Houdini had made on him at close range. "He talks incessantly and never seems to know when to stop. He seemed just a little—well, the sort of person who would get on my nerves if I had to meet him often. But my hat is off to him as a performer. It took genius to do what he did last night. Eight splendid feats, each one more incredible than its predecessor. The illusion he created was unbelievable. He has a magnificent stage presence—I've never seen anything that could remotely compare with it. He was absolutely confident, and dominated the audience from first to last, without dispelling the way they must have felt—that he was taking unjustified risks with his life. That was a very difficult thing to do. He had to create two contradictory impressions—that he could succeed in freeing himself beyond any possibility of doubt, and that his confidence was unshaken in that respect. But he also had to make the audience feel that total failure could not be ruled out, and that he was heroically aware of the danger.

"Feats of that nature are always spectacularly sensational and are tailored to appeal to what is most credulous in the popular mind. I was almost certain that the performance would have a certain aspect of cheapness, even of clownishness about it. It would have possessed such an aspect, I'm sure, if anyone but Houdini had been on that stage. But there was nothing meretricious about it—no, I mustn't say what I would have been tempted to say for a moment last night. All such performances are meretricious because they are faked—absurd and exaggerated in every respect. But he made it all seem genuine while you were looking at it, and my hat is off to him, as I've said."

Henneberger meanwhile had been hoping that HPL would not turn down the editorship offer when it came, and there were many moments when Howard remained on the verge of accepting. But just the thought of residing in Chicago, a city totally lacking in all the traditional associations which were of supreme importance, made him realize that he was "dreaming dreams that could not be." There may be nothing wrong with such a pastime ordinarily, but when the dreams threaten to turn into a hideous nightmare and take on form and substance, it is much wiser to put a quick and decisive end to them. He informed Henneberger that while he would be happy to take over the editorship if some arrangement could be worked out that would permit him to edit the magazine by mail from Providence, or even from Brooklyn, his residence in the Windy City would be out of the question.

"*Chicago!*" I can still hear him saying. "Think of what just one month in that dreadful metropolis would do to the old gentleman! When Sandburg called it 'Hog Butcher For the World,' he thought he was paying it a compliment, which is what you'd expect of a decadent urban poet. He wouldn't have the remotest idea of how *I* would feel if I came within fifty blocks of the stockyards. The Fulton Street fish market is bad enough, and as for the buildings—you can be just as much outraged by total newness, stripped of all aesthetic meaning. Chicago is a bare, bleak, hideous city."

It did no good for me to remind him that he had not confirmed this for himself at first hand. "There might be many things about Chicago you'd like if you paid it just one brief visit. It would cost very little. You could be back in three or four days. Editing that kind of magazine would enable you to double its more discriminating readership. You could transform the entire contents, turn it into a magazine that would be taken much more seriously. And it would relieve you of the financial strain you've been under. If Henneberger had offered me the editorship, I'd be in Chicago next week."

"Perhaps I could persuade him that would be an excellent idea," Howard said. "But if I did, I know what would happen—"

"He'd never give it a serious thought," I said, before he could go on. "I'm not only too young—he would be far less impressed by my stories."

"I wouldn't say you were too young to edit a pulp magazine. And you have a much too modest opinion of your stories. If I showed him just two or three of them, I doubt if I would need to exercise an old gentleman's feeble capacity for eloquence to convince him you would make a splendid editor. But I was thinking of something quite different."

"I guess you may as well tell me."

"You'd become very excited, make all kinds of plans. But you'd never carry them out. I know you too well. You'd be no more capable of packing a suitcase, boarding a train, and securing lodgings in some dismal Chicago rooming house than I would. You're too much attached to your family and you like this decadent metropolis too much—the Village parties, your Casanova-like carryings on, and on a more sensible plane, the American Museum and the Forty-second Street Library. The few compensating rural-vistas and historical survivals that are—or should be—an imperishable part of your heritage seem of less absorbing interest to you."

A week or so later Howard and Henneberger rang the doorbell of the Long apartment and Howard introduced him, followed by a whispered aside to me that he had taken the liberty of inviting him to be our dinner guest.

Henneberger was as unlike HPL as any two individuals of about the same height and hair coloration could possibly be. Henneberger was as highly energized in an extroverted, successful-businessman way as anyone I had met up to that time. He was soft-spoken and had a cultivated, widely-read side to his nature, but he kept it almost entirely under wraps and his conversation during the entire course of the evening centered around the importance of at least tripling the circulation of *Weird Tales* and proceeding from there to build a publishing empire that would dwarf MacFadden's in four or five years. He had lost one fortune in attempting to do just that, and since his efforts in this direction had been to some extent impressive, including the founding of *College Humor,* the possibility he might go even further on another try could not be ruled out.

He was on a brief trip to New York, hoping to raise some badly needed funds for both *Weird Tales* and *Detective Tales,* and had apparently not completely abandoned his efforts to persuade HPL to become a kind of living capital asset at the helm of perhaps more than one of his magazines. Howard, as always, was too kindly disposed to dash all of his hopes totally on that particular evening, and sensible enough to say nothing at all about what he had suggested to me earlier.

With about ten days to think everything over, I found myself entirely in agreement with Howard; if I had jumped at the offer of a *Weird Tales* editorship it would not have been the kind of jump that would have carried me to Chicago. I could picture myself writing Henneberger a long letter of apology the following day, explaining how impossible it would be for me not to tender my resignation, even though I had been an editor for no more than ten or twelve hours. And I could even visualize the kind of letter I would have received in reply.

In the course of the evening Howard did something far more sensible. He talked Henneberger into sending two of my stories to Baird. One was my first *Weird Tales* story, *The Desert Lich,* and the other a straight detective tale. Baird accepted the detective tale a week afterward and asked me to send him a photograph and a brief biographical sketch, which I did. A short while later *Detective Tales* was sold, and both the photo and the sketch were returned to me, along with the galley proofs for the story…the printer had lost the manuscript. Baird then turned *The Desert Lich* over to the new editor of *Weird Tales,* Farnsworth Wright.

CHAPTER TEN

All reputable dictionaries define a saga as: One—an Old Norse story of heroic deeds; Two—any modern heroic narrative. There would be no need to extend the second definition metaphorically in order to embrace a detailed account of the major contributions to HPL's fame by the magazine *Weird Tales* and, posthumously, by Arkham House.

Heroic deeds accompanied every stage of HPL's progression from obscurity to fame: by Farnsworth Wright, the editor of *Weird Tales,* who could so easily have shared the views of several other, less courageous editors who feared that HPL's stories might be lacking in popular appeal; by HPL himself, who refused to compromise his artistic integrity by writing a single line with a newsstand magazine audience in mind; and by August Derleth and Donald Wandrei, who rescued almost all of HPL's macabre fiction from threatened oblivion after his death. The publication of these stories by Arkham House was indeed Norse-like in its adventurousness, and summons up an image of two Icelandic navigators at the helm of a Viking ship, braving uncharted seas.

In April 1923, just one year after Howard's first visit to New York, he submitted five stories to *Weird Tales*: *The Hound, Dagon, The Statement of Randolph Carter, The Cats of Ulthar,* and *Arthur Jermyn.* His manuscripts were accompanied by a letter that no editor could possibly have read without amazement, or at the very least, a feeling of stunned incredulity.

At that time the magazine was edited by Edwin F. Baird, who was far more interested in detective fiction than stories of supernatural horror, and who in any case was soon to be succeeded by Farnsworth Wright. Baird had read widely in many fields, however, and was a very able editor possessing a keen awareness of the vast gulfs which might exist, not just between a good story and a bad one, but between genuine literary excellence and the sort of mediocre offering which all editors are compelled to accept occasionally when nothing better is available.

There can be little doubt that Baird must have thought HPL's work excellent, for the covering letter would have ordinarily made an instant rejection inevitable. Howard went out of his way to castigate editors in general, not only for a total lack of discrimination, but for committing the unforgivable sin of changing so much as a single line of a story submitted by a writer of high artistic integrity. That such integrity should be perceptible at a glance was not open to question, he contended, and it was the unconscionable tampering with manuscripts by editors that was largely responsible for the deplorable state of contemporary American letters. If Baird could not see to publish the stories exactly as written, their return by the next post would be greatly appreciated.

Baird did return the stories, but only with the plea that Howard retype them, for the single-spacing would not have permitted him to make the few necessary interlineations of a wholly typographical nature which were intended solely for the printer and thus totally unrelated to the literary content.

Typing for Howard was always the most dreaded of ordeals when it did not relate to his correspondence—typewritten letters he managed to turn out with far better grace because they were so few in number—but there can be no doubt that the prospect of seeing five of his stories in the early issues of the magazine supplied sufficient incentive to make compliance with Baird's request seem not too great a hardship. (He told me so in one of his few typewritten letters, which I still possess and which stands out as a rarity amidst hundreds of handwritten ones.)

Baird accepted the stories the instant they were returned to him, accompanied by a letter of praise that must have given Howard no small amount of pleasure, although there is no reference to that in his next letter to me. It is on record, however, that when engaged in correspondence with Baird a short while later, he described his disenchantment with every aspect of human existence not intimately associated with memories dating back to his childhood, just as he did when writing to his much closer friends and correspondents, including myself.

Weird Tales was so different from the other pulp magazines of the period and played so important a role in Howard's ascent to fame across the years that some words are in order here concerning its uniqueness. I could do no better than to quote a few paragraphs which appeared in *WT50 (*Robert Weinberg, ed., *WT50* [Oak Lawn, Illinois: privately printed, 1974]) a tribute to the magazine on its fiftieth anniversary:

"In the heyday of the pulp magazines," I wrote, "it was not too remarkable a feat for an all-fiction publication with a distinctly limited audience appeal to avoid disaster for a great many years. But what is remarkable about *Weird Tales* is the 'living legend' aspect which it has taken on today, when it has ceased to appear on the newsstands and close to half a century has gone by since an early issue made H. P. Lovecraft decide that he had perhaps found an audience for his genius-inspired tales of fantasy and horror.

"I have often found myself wondering what it was that enveloped *Weird Tales* in such an extended burst of glory, so to speak, and believe I may have arrived at the answer. Very few of the contributors whose work is remembered today thought of themselves as popular magazine writers. Not a few of them went so far as to believe they were what used to be known as 'literary men,' or 'Men of Letters.' That is considered a very old-fashioned, snobbish term today and writers in general shy away from applying it to themselves and to others. I am quite sure that even Norman Mailer prefers to think of himself as a tough-fibered, hard-bitten 'regular guy' and would flee from such a label with a backward glance of derision, branding it a Victorian hangup.

"But the term did have great validity at one time—when HPL was in his thirties—and it possessed such validity for Clark Ashton Smith, August Derleth, Tennessee Williams (whose first published story appeared in *Weird Tales),* Ray Bradbury, Robert Bloch, Henry Kuttner, C. L. Moore, Theodore Sturgeon, Donald and Howard Wandrei, and a half-dozen other *Weird Tales* contributors I could mention.

"Anyway, what I am trying to say is that the early and middle period *Weird Tales* contributors whose work has survived today were in all respects the exact opposite of pulp magazine writers. But they were, for the most part, quite young, and there was absolutely no other magazine in America as receptive to the kind of stories they preferred to write. (The so-called 'slicks' such as *Collier's* and *Saturday Evening Post* very seldom published fantasy or horror stories, and that was virtually true also of *Harper's* or the *Atlantic*.) And Farnsworth Wright, despite his editorial blind spots—and he had several—was an extremely discerning editor.

"Some of the early contributors have since abandoned fantasy, supernatural horror story, and science fiction writing and carved distinguished careers for themselves in other fields. A few, like Chatterton, died at an early age, 'perishing in their pride.' Others have turned to mainstream fiction—if one wishes to cling to the unjustified assumption that serious literature in any genre can be thought of as outside the mainstream—or have somehow managed to become successful physicists, biochemists, engineers, musicians, and even abstract painters.

"But August Derleth continued to write weird fiction, despite his fame as a regional novelist. (His *Mr. George,* which appeared in *Weird Tales* under a pen name, Stephen Grendon, has been frequently anthologized and dramatized on television. But the most memorable thing about that story is the aura of literary greatness which hovers over every line, making it, in my estimation, one of the two or three most outstanding tales in the entire genre, comparable only to Henry James' *The Turn of the Screw* in its subtle, somber, terrifying capture of those ghostly, nursery-period encroachments which imaginative children are sometimes called upon to overcome.) And Donald Wandrei has never stopped being enthralled by supernatural horror in its more cosmic aspects; his novel *The Web of Easter Island* and his many short stories will be remembered, I think, for many years to come.

"Robert Bloch now has not only *Psycho,* but two other major film productions to his credit, and has become perhaps America's Number One Horror Expert. And Ray Bradbury enjoys both a popular and a serious literary reputation exceeding that of any other writer in the field. He has written at least twenty stories on the imperishable, literary-heritage level.

"As for HPL—the literary recognition which has accrued since his death has placed him on a higher pedestal than the one occupied by Bierce, and it can be predicted, with a fair measure of confidence, that he will soon stand at Poe's side on the highest supernatural story pedestal of all, if he is not already there."

(My quotation from the above text has been amplified just a little, for in the period since its publication some thoughts have come to me which were absent from my mind when I wrote it—by no means an unusual occurrence. I have also omitted several paragraphs concerning two other almost equally legendary pulp magazines, John W. Campbell's *Unknown* and *Astounding Science Fiction,* because they have no very direct or important bearing on the much longer life span of *Weird Tales.)*

The *Weird Tales* saga in retrospect has a kind of immediateness for me even today, because I was so involved with it on a personal, if not I fear a particularly heroic, level. It required no special display of heroism for me to write and sell thirty-five stories to the magazine, for by some strange coincidence Wright had usually run out of rejection slips when one of my stories arrived (or so he implied on two or three occasions), and it was very easy for me to take him at his word. And though the very small sum I received for the stories—one cent a word—was always welcome, I was in no danger of starving to death if *Weird Tales* collapsed, or Wright decided that he had made a mistake in praising my first two or three submissions so extravagantly. He was sincere to a fault, and I have always remained convinced that what he wrote me about *The Desert Lich* and *Death Waters,* which he placed on one of the early covers with an illustration by Brosnatch, was in accord with the way he actually felt about the stories. But a certain number of them he may well have accepted almost by rote, with an "Oh, well—" attitude. He did agree with me that *A Visitor from Egypt, The Black Druid,* and *Second Night Out* (published under its original title, *The Black, Dead Thing*), were my three best stories; so it is difficult for me to fault his critical judgment in certain, areas. And I shall always remain grateful to him for not rejecting more than four stories at most—I am uncertain as to the exact number.

Toward Howard's stories he adopted a somewhat different attitude. His admiration for them verged upon idolatry, and he clearly felt that if *Weird Tales* failed to contain three or four Lovecraft stories in the course of a year, there would ensue a reader disappointment of a very serious nature. This made him rather cautious and unduly fearful, for the thought appears to have crossed his mind more than once that a reputation so firmly established had to be scrupulously guarded. The mere possibility that HPL might once or twice happen to write a story that was no better than four-fifths of the other work he was accepting made him reject several of the later, and very great stories.

He honestly felt that they did not measure up to some of HPL's earlier, shorter tales in dramatic suspense and one or two other qualities. He did not reject them primarily because of their length, even though he may well have taken this into consideration. Later he changed his mind and accepted them. But he should not have rejected them the first time, in view of some of the very terrible stories that he sometimes felt the readers might like for one reason or another.

In a number of letters to me and to several other correspondents, Howard became as bitterly disappointed as I had ever known him to be, and said some exceedingly caustic things about Wright. But I do not believe he ever really meant them. Basically I think he was very fond of Wright and had a high respect for him both as a man of generous impulses and as an editor. But Wright did have some blind spots, and Howard was placed in a position of being forced to make the best of just one editor's opinion when a story which he *knew* was superior to all of his earlier work came back with a graciously phrased letter of rejection. It was a grievous blow to him, despite the gracious phrasing.

"I'll never send him another story," Howard told me. "He has every right to reject the story if he doesn't like it. But I know now that he never will like any of my stories. Not from this point on. Nothing I'll write in the future will be any different from my more recent stories. The creation of a certain atmosphere through the slow, cumulative piling up of minute, realistic detail means nothing to him. All he wants is a stereotyped stressing of the gruesome. He wants me to go back and write as I once did. *And that I will not do.*"

In a quite early letter Howard referred to Wright as "a mediocre Chicago writer," but that judgment was based upon one of Wright's own stories—and only one—which was hardly a masterpiece in the horror story genre. Later Howard considerably revised his feelings toward Wright, for he soon discovered that the editor of *Weird Tales* was a well-read, highly imaginative man with a wide range of cultivated interests, including music criticism. But when the second of those two rejections occurred, he was seriously tempted to revert to his earlier feelings about "that new editor whom Henneberger has chosen to replace Baird, hoping he'll make some changes which will increase its circulation and, of course, utterly rule out the possibility that it will contain at least a few stories of genuine artistic merit."

But the explosion I had witnessed after Wright's second rejection dated from a later period and was only briefly duplicated in the letters by an outpouring of ungenerous comments. Howard was incapable of being critical for very long before his innate sense of fairness emphatically reasserted itself. A short while later he wrote me that he had always felt that Wright deserved a great deal of credit for having published the work of at least six writers of exceptional talent who were far less popular with the readers than an equal number of less gifted writers.

Howard never thought of himself as—or would have wanted to be—a professional writer. I am absolutely certain he never wrote a line that was altered to the slightest extent by monetary considerations. To write to sell was for him an almost degrading occupation, which he could forgive his friends for regarding as somewhat of a necessity but which he could never have forgiven in himself. Had he deliberately set out to be a professional writer, I am quite certain he would have made a success of it, despite everything in his nature to the contrary: his occasional periods of extreme indolence which I suppose the uncharitable would equate with laziness, his inability to conquer completely his letter-writing impulsiveness, and his difficulty in channeling all of his energies in an efficient, business-like way to achieve just one goal to the exclusion of everything else. The pleasure principle was important to him, as it should be to every civilized human being, and to put it completely aside for the sake of long-range planning, as the more obtuse or emotionally distorted psychiatrists advise, would have seemed to him unthinkable, despite his New England work-ethic heritage. And a professional writer must do that at times, or perish.

But I still think that had he deliberately set out to be a highly successful professional writer he would have done well at it. His stories, all apart from the qualities which made them so contributory to the enrichment of human experience on a higher level than that of mere entertainment, were sufficiently suspenseful in their plot structure and contained enough dramatic confrontations, even if on a cosmic plane, to provide a great deal of entertainment. His only problem, which I know he could have surmounted, would have been to write ten times as many stories and send each one out a dozen or more times, if necessary, until some discerning editor realized that the rejection of a Lovecraft story would have been an act of folly. And it would have involved also a constant bickering with editors on a wholly commercial basis and a willingness to make suggested changes. This would have been repugnant to him, but I am convinced he could have accomplished it had he really wished to do so. The only problem was—he did not wish to.

It was an inhibiting factor which is far from absent in myself. But when one *has* to do something, it is amazing how often all such inhibitions can be broken down by some mysterious, unconscious process which makes suicidal behavior unappealing.

I do not believe Howard gave a thought to what a rejection meant in terms of economic deprivation, tremendously welcome as even a small check would have been to him at all times. But just the fact that he knew Wright was far from totally lacking in sound artistic judgment made him feel that there might just possibly be something about the story that had made a rejection justifiable. Few writers can avoid thinking along these lines at times, unless their confidence in their own work is prodigious and their contempt for all editorial opinion provides them with an impregnable shield. Howard possessed no such emotional armor-plating, for he was the most remorseless of self-critics and seriously felt on occasion that he had failed totally to recapture, in even the best of his stories, the tremendous vistas of cosmic strangeness and wonder that haunted his dreams.

He was not for an instant unaware of Wright's fallibility, and he knew as well, in a profoundly unassailable way, that this editor could never have written a story remotely comparable to the work he most admired. But that did not mean that Wright was not a highly sensitive and imaginative man, or that even among the readers of *Weird Tales* there would not be, here and there, a man or woman who would know whether he had succeeded or failed and would judge him by standards that were worthy of respect.

There were always a few such readers; and although he did not write with a magazine audience in mind but solely for the kind of aesthetic satisfaction which writing provided him, he could still be made to feel, through editorial or reader response alone, that he had failed. For many of the crudely-phrased, wholly immature readers' comments which appeared in "The Eyrie," the letter column of *Weird Tales,* he quite justifiably had no respect whatsoever. But there were other comments which, if they had been severely critical of a Lovecraft story, would have produced such a feeling, and by increasing his self-doubt would have caused him distress. Fortunately there were few, if any, such comments. From every stratum of the readership—and since it was the only magazine in America devoted entirely to fantasy and horror the strata were wide and varied—there arose paeans of praise. Then as now, HPL had a multi-level readership, though it was limited to just one magazine.

Jacques Bergier has discussed HPL's stories in relation to *Weird Tales* specifically in *Histoire des literatures, (*Raymond Queneau, ed., *Histoire des litteratures* [Paris: Gallimard, 1956], vol. 3, p. 1678.) stressing the irony of that relationship when viewed in the light of his current fame, since *Weird Tales* was, after all, a pulp magazine. He adds that it was also an embarrassment in a literary sense to Bradbury, since many of his finest stories appeared in the same publication. But there is, I believe, a lack of understanding here.

The pulp magazines of the period extended over a wide range, and the worst of them were on a very low level indeed. But the best of the pulps, *Adventure, Short Stories,* and *Blue Book,* published much fiction which was superior stylistically and in other ways to the average slick-paper magazine story of the 1920s and early 1930s. Many of the stories in *Collier's* and *Saturday Evening Post* forty years ago were atrociously written, and not a few would seem laughable today—cliché-ridden, naive, with formulaic plots and Pollyanna-ish characterization. *Harper's, The Century, The Atlantic Monthly,* and some of the small literary journals were of course on a much higher level; but there also were stories of equal stature in the best of the pulps, to such an extent that at least a dozen of the foremost writers of the period were not ashamed to appear occasionally in their pages. Sinclair Lewis had a few stories in the pulps; T. S. Stribling, a Pulitzer prize winning novelist, was a frequent contributor to *Adventure*; Cornell Woolrich (William Irish) appeared in the detective magazines; and Luke Short, the most realistic and stylistically accomplished western story writer, was a pulp author for ten or twelve years before he made the "slicks," to cite just four examples.

Of course *Weird Tales* was a pulp magazine of uneven quality, with extremely lurid covers. Some of the stories were quite terrible, crudely melodramatic and so hackneyed in phraseology that they would have been thought cliché-ridden even if written a century earlier. But in the unusual factors which I have stressed in the *WT50* article, I think that Bergier would have found the answer to the problem which troubled him. It was no more incongruous for HPL to grace the pages of *Weird Tales* than for a writer of established literary reputation forty years ago to write occasionally for two or three of the better pulp magazines.

If one goes back to the 1840s, he will find a more striking incongruity; some of the magazines for which Poe wrote such as *Godey's Lady's Book,* which were considered at that time to have been prestigious literary journals, inflicted upon their readers thousands of pages of gaslight-era trash. Even the worst pulp magazines of the 1920s were at least slightly superior to many of the 1840 era publications which had a general, if not precisely literary, readership. Poe, Hawthorne, and the other distinguished mid-nineteenth century authors were all too aware of those inanities, yet had no choice but to pretend otherwise, for what other contemporary American publications could they have pointed to for purposes of comparison? Poe did not wholly pretend, and criticized some of them with unsparing vigor. But a story by Poe or Hawthorne could have appeared in all of them without causing, from the modern viewpoint of a Harvard professor of literature, the slightest raising of eyebrows, for the inanities of the past have to some extent become hallowed by a long forgetting.

One thing is certain: there has been no great decline in *popular* taste today in the realm of fiction, all apart from literature, despite television and every other modern encroachment. In a few areas it has become fifty times more perceptive than it was in 1840.

Incidentally, it is worth noting that there has been a revival of interest in the pulps today on a serious academic level, both those dating back half a century, and those of as late a period as the mid-1940s. There are eight or ten university libraries with very large pulp magazine collections and biographical material concerning the writers in their archives. To such an extent is this material coveted that more than one writer of my acquaintance whose early stories are remembered today has received competitive bids from several universities for as much source material—original manuscripts with revisions, letters from editors, and similar documents—as it would be possible for anyone to assemble from attic trunks without becoming helplessly entangled in cobwebs. I have been twice thus honored myself, and although in that particular sphere of revived historical interest I feel that my early pulp magazine stories are quite unlike my writing in the book field in recent years and less worthy of preservation than they might have been if I had been less financially harassed, I could hardly have failed to be pleased and flattered by a dignified, highly scholarly letter from a university curator of manuscripts.

CHAPTER ELEVEN

The saga of *Weird Tales* began a short while before HPL submitted his initial offerings to this publication, accompanied by that extraordinary covering letter to Edwin F. Baird. But it was the succession of his stories, one after the other, during the ensuing fifteen years that became a saga which was in some respects without parallel in the domain of magazine fiction. When has there ever been such a fabulous collection of titles in just one genre, and not a genre which at the time was likely to encourage writers to submit material of both genius-level inspiration and yet so utterly indifferent to commercial considerations?

The titles alone read like a procession of eerily illuminated, wraith-like lines of lettering passing in spectral review, such as might greet the eye of some desert wayfarer who had stumbled upon a dark tower of wonderment and entered it in fear and trembling with a forbidden key which he had just uncovered outside in the sand: *The Quest of Iranon, The Festival, The Cats of Ulthar, The Tomb, The Call of Cthulhu, Pickman's Model, The Strange High House in the Mist, The Silver Key, The Dunwich Horror, The Whisperer in Darkness, The Dreams in the Witch-House, The Haunter of the Dark*, and others.

Among his published stories there are three which, at least to me, have always seemed the greatest of all. One of them, *At the Mountains of Madness,* appeared in another magazine, and I shall discuss it at some length along with *The Shunned House* when I deal with the Arkham House saga, because only this publisher assembled all of his stories and accorded them hardcover permanence.

A critical analysis, or even a brief plot summary of just a portion of his early and middle period stories would, of necessity, occupy too many pages to justify such an undertaking in the present volume. Even the author of a full-length biography would have to exercise considerable vigilance and restraint in that respect.

The stories themselves are now so readily obtainable elsewhere, both in hardcover and paperback editions, that no sensible purpose would be served by thematic summaries, regardless of their brevity. But something nevertheless must be said here about the stories as Howard himself viewed them, for that bears a direct relationship to my many talks with him and should not be omitted from a memoir. And it involves as well, I fear, summaries of at least three or four works that came close to achieving what he most wanted to accomplish—the transference to paper of an actual dream experience with little, if any, distortion. No story he ever wrote gave him complete satisfaction, but I am sure he knew when one *almost* did.

Of the quite large number of his Dunsanian period tales, not more than two or three made him feel, upon rereading them in later years, that they were worth preserving; I think he regretted that some had even been published and would not have minded seeing them sink into oblivion. But he did not feel this way about *The Nameless City* which he enclosed with a letter in the third year of our correspondence (it did not appear in *Weird Tales* until 1938), and which I carried about with me in my freshman year at NYU, reread frequently, and showed to everyone whom I could talk into sharing my admiration for it. (It was on glossy yellow paper, single-spaced, and ended up badly crumpled. But the color of the paper at least, would have prevented it from turning more yellowish with the years—it could not have been a brighter yellow.)

The other two Dunsanian period stories which Howard considered the best writing of which he had been capable at that particular time were *The Doom That Came to Sarnath* and *The Cats of Ulthar*—perhaps chiefly because cats vied with Dunsany's *The Book of Wonder* in lending enchantment to every "Edge of the World" landscape that haunted his dreams. *The Statement of Randolph Carter* embodied a dream experience which made it seem of supreme importance to him at the time, but he told me around 1933 that he no longer cared for it. *The Doom That Came to Sarnath* was one of the very few of Howard's stories I never saw in manuscript, but later he mentioned it several times and assured me it was among the three or four of his Dunsanian period tales he would not have objected to having Wright publish, if any of these stories really *had* to be published.

He always agreed with me that the later, extended tales were superior to all of his shorter fiction. But there were four of the middle period stories that he may have liked almost as well, although he sometimes denied this. These were *The Colour out of Space, The Music of Erich Zann, Pickman's Model,* and of course, *The Dunwich Horror. The Call of Cthulhu* preceded the latter and was even more central to the Mythos, but this is the single Mythos tale that has never commanded my enthusiasm, and Howard told me more than once that he personally much preferred *The Dunwich Horror.* There were others almost as great, notably *The Whisperer in Darkness* and *The Shadow Over Innsmouth,* the latter having been published posthumously in *Weird Tales* but earlier as a hardcover book.

The Colour out of Space appeared in another magazine and hence is not strictly part of the *Weird Tales* saga. But since it is one of the middle period stories which came very close to making Howard feel he had achieved the mood synthesis which he had set as his goal from the beginning, and as it bears a close categorical relationship to the other three, I have thought it best to discuss all of them here in sequence.

As suggested by its title, *The Colour out of Space* deals with a cosmic intrusion upon the world of familiar scenes and events. This "colour" was calculated to drive the beholder totally mad, since like the wholly alien, terrifying harmonies in *The Music of Erich Zann,* it could not be thought of as a sense-impression that had anything in common with ordinary sounds or colors. It was rather the sort of alien phenomenon that so far transcended what Wordsworth seems to have had in mind when he wrote of "the light that never was on sea or land," that it existed in a galactic universe apart, but had somehow managed to escape from its multidimensional matrix and arrive on earth in an active, and devastatingly destructive guise. It has a destroying capacity that can only be compared to the heat that smoulders at the core of first magnitude suns, except that it was no more like heat in the ordinarily understood sense than it was like terrestrial sound or color. In this, perhaps more than in any of his other stories long or short, HPL succeeded in conveying a feeling of such total alienage that from the first page to the last the reader is not even called upon to exercise a suspension of disbelief. That suspension is imposed hypnotically by the theme itself and by the words that flowed from HPL's mind to the paper which must surely have wavered a little now and then as the "colour" threatened to seep into its very texture and demolish it.

In *The Music of Erich Zann* a strange, gnome-like little man fiddles away at music just as unearthly; as it swells in volume and intensity the house itself begins to tilt and careen in a dizzying vortex of horror. It becomes music so terrifyingly cosmic, so alien to human ears that there remains no sane way of describing it and we are swept inexorably into a multidimensional realm of nightmarish destructiveness in which the toppling of just one room or one house fades into insignificance beside the toppling of the universe of stars.

In *Pickman's Model* the encroachments are just a little less cosmic, for they deal with earthbound monsters of a somewhat Frankensteinian character. (I shall let stand here, for the sake of descriptive convenience, a long established inaccuracy, for Frankenstein was, of course, not the monster, but simply its creator!). But although they are monsters from hidden crypts associated with the burial vaults of old and decaying families, there is more than a hint of cosmic suggestiveness about them as well. The young artist whose morbidity is perhaps unique in the entire realm of the macabre is one of HPL's most memorable characterizations: he is depicted as both compulsive beyond belief and a defiant and fearless artist rebel. (Despite what has often been said to the contrary, HPL could often excel in characterization, although that gift never enabled him to bring to life prosaic, run-of-the-mill individuals.) It is easy to understand his liking for that story, since it was as successful an evocation of mood as he might have wished—or almost as successful. Only his striving for absolute perfection in all his stories could have prevented him from having a few slight reservations about it, and, as I told him more than once, they were reservations which I could not share. Of its kind, I have never read a story more utterly compelling.

Apart from *At the Mountains of Madness* and *The Shunned House, The Dunwich Horror* seemed to him the most satisfying of his stories, and that self-appraisal I have never had the slightest inclination to question, either in what I told him immediately after its publication in *Weird Tales,* or in recent years when my critical judgment has undergone considerable maturing.

The Dunwich Horror is predominantly a tale of monstrous family degeneration, linking it to several of his earlier, shorter stories on the same theme, but embracing aspects of cosmic horror uniquely Lovecraftian in their myth-making potential. In this story the Old Ones are present as a kind of background waltz macabre, accompanied by a full-scale foreground orchestration in which the Whateley twins, one hidden for years from the outside world and the other a troubled youth of great scholastic brilliance, play out their roles to a shuddering, unforgettable climax.

Although stories such as these are now considered milestones in the saga of *Weird Tales,* there were several other contributors to the magazine who were capable of producing work of exceptional literary quality, some of which was comparable to the best of HPL's stories. But with the exception of Clark Ashton Smith and Henry S. Whitehead (many of Donald Wandrei's best stories appeared elsewhere, while Ray Bradbury was not an early contributor and wrote more extensively for other magazines), none of them were as prolific as Howard or maintained so consistently a high level of excellence in the domain of both the macabre and the cosmically fabulous over so long a period of time. August Derleth's very early tales which he wrote at the age of seventeen were not comparable to his later *Weird Tales* stories, and his greatest, most memorable contributions to the genre were, of course, the Arkham House Cthulhu Mythos collaborations which HPL never lived to see and which have contributed in no small measure to HPL's worldwide fame.

The way HPL felt about the poetry, stories, drawings, and sculpture of Clark Ashton Smith is so widely on record both in his letters and elsewhere, that there is no need here for me to discuss these works. Just one quotation from an early HPL letter should suffice, since it goes to the very core of what it was in Smith's stories which convinced HPL that no other writer shared his approach to "a wild weird clime that lieth, sublime, out of space—out of time" to quite the same extent. And other realms as well, as the quotation makes evident.

"No author but yourself," he wrote to Smith in 1923, "seems to have glimpsed fully those tenebrous wastes, immeasurable gulfs, grey topless pinnacles, crumbling corpses of forgotten cities, slimy, stagnant, cypress-bordered rivers, and alien, indefinable, antiquity-ridden gardens of strange decay with which my own dreams have been crowded since earliest childhood." (H. P. Lovecraft, *Selected Letters 1,* ed. by August Derleth and Donald Wandrei [Sauk City:

Arkham House, 1965], p. 213.)

Some reference to CAS, however brief, almost always occurred in the course of a conversation with me concerning the entire *Weird Tales* group, or fantasy writing of a general nature; and on many occasions he would discuss Smith alone for ten or fifteen minutes without pause.

The stories of Henry S. Whitehead, an Episcopalian clergyman living in Florida whom Howard met once and corresponded with at considerable length for several years, are certainly deserving of literary permanence. To what extent they will achieve it is difficult to predict, for though the best of them have been preserved in hardcover by Arkham House in *Jumbee and Other Uncanny Tales* and *West India Lights,* the Reverend Dr. Whitehead was not a writer equal to either HPL or CAS in stature. But he was a very fine scrivener of macabre tales—almost as powerfully evocative, within a smaller compass, as the subtly suggestive, artistically restrained ghost stories of M. R. James. Aside from his skillful avoidance of all overwriting, Whitehead was a master at conjuring up ghostly presences peculiar to the West Indies—darkly malignant, tomb-dwelling entities, either as attenuated as a wisp of smoke surviving from some ancient funeral-pyre ceremony by supernatural means, or so small and hobbling that they could easily be mistaken for toads walking upright by some beholder with very poor eyesight. There are strange lights and echoes from the long-buried past, where that which is hoary with age embraces the zombie-like survivors of more recent and unhallowed occurrences in a mad waltz above Voodoo-cursed graves.

Whitehead's long residence in the West Indies and his familiarity with the scenes he describes give all of his stories an atmospheric validity which, as a regional writer with an accomplished style as well, he could scarcely have failed to achieve. I once told Howard that HSW seemed to know the West Indies better than nine out of ten of the travel book writers who had made that region their most frequently visited port of call, and Howard went a little further and revised my appraisal to eliminate all competing writers in Whitehead's chosen field.

"No one who writes about the West Indies could hope to excel if its ghostly, legend-haunted survivals from the remote past failed to stir his imagination in much the same way that Providence stirs mine, from its ancient steeples to its cypress-shadowed graveyards, with the waning sunlight slanting down over tombs tilted in a blasphemously-angled way."

"Except that West Indian ghosts are quite different from Providence ones," I once reminded him. "And you don't believe in ghosts anyway. Does Whitehead, I wonder?"

"Naturally not. But what difference does that make? It's the suggestive atmosphere I'm talking about—the creation of a *mood.*"

CHAPTER TWELVE

Although the Arkham House saga has extended over an even longer number of years, it has displayed a remarkably consistent quality throughout its history. Since there has been no deviation from the publisher's early established goals, we do not need to pursue its course along footpaths where the dragons of mediocrity crouch at every turn, for it contains no such dismal, swamp-infested areas whatsoever.

That saga, too, is amply on record elsewhere, and is in fact essential to every aspect of HPL's posthumous fame aside from the stories themselves. But though I have pursued the policy of not quoting directly from previous Arkham House books, an exception must be made this one time, for all retellings of that saga elsewhere are lacking in the eloquent simplicity and directness with which the founding of Arkham House and its growth across the years have been described in *Thirty Years of Arkham House* by August Derleth himself:

"When Howard Wandrei, then in New York, wrote to tell me that Lovecraft had died, I read his letter on my way into the marshes below Sauk City, where I frequently went to sit in the sun and read, and where that day I had along a volume of Thoreau's *Journal*. Instead of reading, however, I sat at a railroad trestle beside a brook and thought of how Lovecraft's best stories could be published in book form...

"Later that day I wrote Donald Wandrei that something should be done to keep Lovecraft's fine stories in print... There was never any question about the name of the publishing house—the imprint to be used on what we then thought perhaps the first of three volumes. *Arkham House* suggested itself at once, since it was Lovecraft's own well-known, widely used place-name for legend-haunted Salem, Massachusetts, in his remarkable fiction; it seemed to us that this was fitting and that Lovecraft himself would have approved of it enthusiastically. And, once the project was decided upon, there was never any doubt about the printer chosen to do it—we turned at once to the nearest, most widely known printer who could do a complete operation—the George Banta Company of Menasha, Wisconsin, whose plant was only a trifle over a hundred miles northeast of Sauk City.

"The first quartet of books to bear the imprint of Arkham House—published from 1939 to 1944—though getting off to a slow selling start with the initial Lovecraft title, had by the end of 1943 gained such momentum that it was obvious that few if any of these books would be left for sale by the end of 1944.

"Since the general domain of the macabre was limited, I felt that it would be necessary, if I meant to enter serious publishing, to effect as much of a 'corner' on the market as possible, and to that end I signed to contracts the foremost authors on both sides of the Atlantic—Algernon Blackwood, L. P. Hartley, Lord Dunsany, Lady Cynthia Asquith, A. E. Coppard, Clark Ashton Smith, Ray Bradbury, A. E van Vogt, Arthur Machen, H. Russell Wakefield, et al…

"The close of the first decade of publishing saw a substantial number of Arkham House titles out of print and selling at fantastic prices…" (August Derleth, *Thirty Years of Arkham House* [Sauk City: Arkham House, 1970], pp. 1-9 passim.)

But in the beginning it took great courage, perseverance, and foresight to get Arkham House established, and both Derleth and Wandrei strained their modest resources to the utmost, making more than one personal sacrifice to ensure that there would be a wide and discriminating audience for HPL's first short story collection in hardcover.

I have tried to convey my feelings about this second and greater of the two sagas in an article, "The Keeper of the Flame," which I recently contributed to *IS,* (Tom Collins, ed., *IS:4* [Meriden, Connecticut: privately printed, 1971].) a publication that devoted eighty-two pages to a memorial tribute to Derleth by eighteen writers and editors. Most of them had known August personally, and not a few like myself were indebted to Arkham House for the kind of literary recognition which only hardcover publication can make possible:

"There is a branch of literature which has never ceased to be in danger of not receiving its rightful due for close to a century and a half, perhaps longer, in both America and Europe. It is the literature of the strange, the wildly fanciful, the terrifying, and, very often, the supremely beautiful. I am not sure, but I believe it was Matthew Arnold who said that enduring works of art become imperishable through the persistent praises of the 'passionate few' at first, sometimes for only a while, but usually for a number of years before their greatness becomes universally recognized.

"That is particularly true of those high flights of human imagination which provide us with rare and resplendent visions of worlds lying just beyond the borderlands of the known, with their high mountain peaks gleaming in the light that never was on sea or land.

"In the realm of pure fantasy and supernatural horror the 'passionate few' have been fewer than in any other branch of literature. For the past thirty years August Derleth had been the chief American guardian of this rare, imperishable flame, and that is the highest tribute that I could pay him on a non-personal level. On a more personal level I can only say that I have lost a friend whose like I never will see again, and his passing has left a void which nothing, I fear, will ever fill."

In 1964 Arkham House published *At the Mountains of Madness and Other Novels* in an omnibus collection which included not only the title work, but also the one other novel which I have always felt was comparable to it in greatness, *The Shunned House.* To my mind *At the Mountains of Madness* has always seemed to tower above nearly all his other writings, though perhaps "tower above" is not precisely the right phrase, for the peaks attained by both *The Shunned House* and *The Case of Charles Dexter Ward* are almost as mighty in stature.

In this long narrative, laid in the Antarctic continent, which had as much fascination for HPL as it did for Poe, a gigantic megalopolis in which dwelt—But no, it would be a mistake for me to continue in this vein; for if I attempted to summarize the novel in my own words, I would totally fail to do justice to its night-shadowed immensities and tremendous cosmic sweep. Only HPL himself would be capable of accomplishing that in just one paragraph. No more is really needed here to convey a sense of just how tremendous the novel is in its entirety, for the following passage is far more than just a summary of narrative events in the order in which they occur.

It omits, in fact, nine-tenths of what a story summary is supposed to contain, for it deals only with a single dread revelation which blazes into a mind-shattering kind of immediacy for the narrator, threatening to topple his sanity and send him fleeing with an inward screaming over an untrodden waste of snow and glacial ice.

> The things once rearing and dwelling in this frightful masonry of the paleogean megalopolis, n the age of dinosaurs were not indeed dinosaurs, but far worse. Mere dinosaurs were new and almost brainless objects—but the builders of the city were wise and old, and had left certain traces on rocks even then laid down well nigh a thousand million years—rocks laid down before the true life of earth had advanced beyond plastic groups of cells—rocks laid down before the true life of earth had existed at all. They were the makers and enslavers of that life… They were the great "Old Ones" that had filtered down from the stars when earth was young—the beings whose substance an alien evolution had shaped and whose powers were such as this planet had never bred.

For me Lovecraft's longer stories have always been the great ones. They build slowly to magnificent climaxes; they are brooding, atmospheric, tapestried with strange colors alien to the world we know in our mundane moments, alien to everything that takes place when we are not dreamers and visionaries and explorers of the great unknown.

The posthumously published *The Case of Charles Dexter Ward* and *At the Mountains of Madness* are surely two of the greatest. *The Shunned House* is similarly magnificent as the tempo of its dread revelations becomes more and more like the conjurations of some baton waver with an orchestra wider than the universe at his command. But the orchestra is merely the instrument of something greater than the dark music itself. The conductor is the creator, building edifices of stone, hoary with age and crumbling before he completes them; and the shrieking that ensues is something quite different from the music, because it is not really sound at all, but something infinitely more wild and strange, some horrifying harmony audible to the inner ear.

There is one other story I would place quite high on the list, *The Shadow out of Time,* which appeared in *Astounding Stories* in 1936. It is powerful indeed, but I cannot agree with certain other critics that it is the best story HPL ever wrote.

CHAPTER THIRTEEN

During HPL's New York period the Kalem Club met at regular intervals, usually twice a month. The members either convened at my residence, or at the homes of Samuel Loveman, Arthur Leeds, or George Kirk. I was the host at the majority of the gatherings, although we assembled at Loveman's Brooklyn Heights apartment perhaps a dozen times.

James F. Morton was present at almost all of the meetings and the instant Howard arrived, an amazing ceremonial ushered in the period of discussion that followed. Morton, whose ruddy-faced geniality had to be witnessed to be believed, would leap to his feet, bow, and intone: "Welcome, most august one. Your scholarly presence now makes our evening complete and brimming over."

"No, it is you, Sir, whose arrival has been most eagerly awaited. It sheds a radiance, a splendor—but words fail me. I shall not feel at ease until I have retreated to an inconspicuous corner, where I may join Belknapius and Samuelus as a silent listener, grateful for words of such oracular wisdom that to impose an interruption would bring down the wrath of the gods."

Almost invariably, however, Howard did most of the talking, at least for the first ten or fifteen minutes. He would sink into an easy chair—he never seemed to feel at ease in a straight-backed chair on such occasions and I took care to keep an extremely comfortable one unoccupied until his arrival—and words would flow from him in a continuous stream.

He never seemed to experience the slightest necessity to pause between words. There was no groping about for just the right term, no matter how recondite his conversation became. When the need for some metaphysical hair-splitting arose, it was easy to visualize scissors honed to a surgical sharpness snipping away in the recesses of his mind.

I doubt whether the classic query of medieval scholastics, "How many angels can dance on the head of a pin?", would have caused him any concern at such moments. He would either have known or refused to stop for ten seconds to dwell upon it.

The meetings seldom broke up before two in the morning and on not a few occasions they lasted until dawn. The refreshments were usually quite simple ones—a tray of cookies and strong coffee, for the most part black. Once or twice my mother baked a cake. My parents remained either in another room of the apartment or chose that particular evening to "take in" some current play or movie. The continuous hum of conversation had a tendency to annoy my father a little, since it was so difficult to shut out even at the other end of the hall. But my mother always accepted it in good grace.

In general the conversation was lively and quite variegated. It was a brilliant enough assemblage, and the discussions ranged from current happenings of a political or sociological nature, to some recent book or play, or to five or six centuries of English and French literature, art, philosophy, and natural science.

But not even Howard's extraordinary presence has made those gatherings seem to me in retrospect to be a great deal different from a thousand and one similar get-togethers of what Christopher Morley—or was it some other columnist?—referred to at the time as "kinsprits," a phrase so memorable that I am ashamed to be a little uncertain as to its origin.

As mentioned earlier, we shared many of the same interests: Loveman was predominantly a poet; James F. Morton a civic-minded public speaker, as well as a mineralogist, sociologist, and liberal arts essayist; Everett McNeil, a juvenile fiction author; George Kirk, a professional book dealer; Arthur Leeds, a short story writer in the adventure field; Wheeler Dryden, a half-brother of Charlie Chaplin who attended about five of those early gatherings; and Rheinhart Kleiner, a very accomplished light versifier who once wrote a poem about Brooklyn which was reprinted in all of the New York papers. "When fate no longer lenient, gives cause to sink and sigh, there's hardly more convenient a place in which to die."

In one respect only did the Kalem Club differ from the many other youthful literary groups scattered about the city at the time: there was never among us any fierce feuding or arguments verging upon the aggressively belligerent. No falling out at all during the period of its existence, which extended from Howard's New York years to long after his return to Providence. Most such groups break apart after four or five years at most, human nature being as it is, but not the Kalems.

The last meeting took place at my home a year after Howard's death and was both a very sad as well as an unforgettable occasion. Farnsworth Wright and Hannes Bok were among the first to arrive, followed by all of the 1920 era members, with the exception of James Morton and Wheeler Dryden. August Derleth was also present, having come to New York to discuss the possible publication of Howard's stories by a major publisher. Vrest Orton, who did not join the group until much later, did not attend that gathering, nor did Wilfred Blanch Talman, to the best of my recollection, but a word is in order here concerning them. Orton was on the staff of the *American Mercury* and knew Mencken and Dreiser quite well; Talman was too young in Howard's New York years to have joined the group at its formation, but he became a very active member in the 1930s. His recently published volume of HPL memories (Wilfred B. Talman, *The Normal Lovecraft* [Saddle River, New Jersey: Gerry de la Ree, 1973].) is outstanding, despite its brevity, and contains not a single inaccurate statement. His memories of Howard are warm and glowing, as they should be, for nothing could be further from the truth than some of the legends that have developed concerning HPL in just the past decade.

That gathering was so well attended that there was less than a square yard of open space in any part of our quite large living room. Farnsworth Wright's Parkinsonism was so far advanced at that period that he stumbled twice and nearly fell. My father was almost moved to tears, he told me later, by the man's tragic and continuous trembling. But Wright always bore up under his affliction with more courage than I would have thought possible; I have never known anyone to display more.

He entered into the spirit of the gathering with a total absence of self-pity. He shared both the grief we all experienced at Howard's passing and the gratitude that enabled us to feel that no greater tribute to HPL's memory could have been arranged. He was a man of discernment who could hold his own in any social gathering, but when there was no need to draw attention to the qualities which he possessed as an editor—there was never, in fact, any such need—he could forget about himself entirely.

It was considerably more than just a memorable occasion. Everyone contributed some memory or appreciation that made HPL seem so indubitably present that it was hard to believe he had not returned as a silent, gray ghost and seated himself in the easy chair he had occupied so many times fifteen years earlier.

August Derleth had never met Howard and knew him only through the many letters that they had exchanged over the years. But to have known HPL through an epistolary relationship was almost the equivalent of having met and talked with him many times in person when the letter writer was August. Like Howard, August had the unique gift of being wholly himself in his letters, and Howard told me more than once that he felt as though he had a more lively and continuous awareness of August as a person than anyone with whom he had ever corresponded. That statement was probably just as true of Alfred Galpin, Donald Wandrei, and myself, but we had met HPL both in person and through correspondence, which makes the tribute unique of its kind. Howard also told me that he felt—and this was quite early in their correspondence—that August would someday be the ambassador of "the gang" to the literary world in general. He told me this at least five years before August acquired anything like his later stature as an important regional novelist, and one of the few writers in America upon whom the mantle of Thoreau has unquestionably descended. (And, to a not inconsiderable extent, as Leslie A. Fiedler once pointed out, the mantle of Whitman as well.)

Unlike Howard, August had no great liking for somberly conventional attire, and on that occasion was wearing what is still known as a polo shirt, along with suspenders which, when he removed his jacket, seemed entirely in harmony with the small town, Wisconsin background which provides authentic source material for his regional novels. In several aspects of his personality August was far from a dyed-in-the-wool Midwesterner. But he could identify with his Sauk City environment with the kind of loving dedication that is inseparable from being born at a certain place and time, experiencing not the slightest need to be a rebel in that particular realm.

It was beyond dispute that his love for Sauk City was both deep and abiding. It could hardly have been otherwise, since it led him to forego many literary gatherings in various parts of the country at which he would have been lionized. He was not without vanity—what writer is?—but Sauk City always meant more to him than literary adulation.

The presence of Hannes Bok at that gathering has, in retrospect, a peculiarly coincidental aspect. August had not met him previously and neither had I. He had read all of HPL's stories; and when Wright introduced him as a new *Weird Tales* artist of exceptional talent, I doubt if even so flattering a comment meant as much to him as just the privilege of being present at a memorial gathering attended by so many of Howard's friends. He was very young at the time, and would have certainly been incredulous if someone had prophetically advised him that he would someday illustrate one of HPL's most powerful stories and do the jacket illustration for my first Arkham House collection of short stories, *The Hounds of Tindalos*.

I have always felt that only Virgil Finlay and Lee Brown Coye were the peers of Bok as macabre fiction illustrators, and occasionally he excelled them both in subtlety and broodingly somber suggestiveness. He was, as Lin Carter has pointed out in a recent Ballantine paperback, unworldly in the extreme, with a boyishness that he never outgrew. But he was boyish in a sophisticated way which enabled him to take delight in many different aspects of human experience, and he was also the happiest individual anyone would be likely to meet.

But I am forgetting that fifteen years would pass before the last of the Kalem gatherings took place and that I am taking liberties with time in an unnecessary way. The first few months which Howard spent in New York were not darkened by a long Shadow out of Time, or any other kind of shadow, and the occasions which stand out most vividly in my memory during those months were comparatively untroubled ones, despite Howard's continuing lack of success in securing employment.

Employment-seeking was, as I have said, an agonizing ordeal for him, but he could banish the thought of it from his mind with remarkable ease when he was in the company of his friends. At least two or three times a week he conducted antiquarian explorations at night, almost always joined by Loveman or Kirk or both. They roamed the Village, the southern tip of Manhattan, and Brooklyn Heights, just looking at old houses and occasionally remaining afoot until dawn.

Although Kleiner shared Howard's antiquarian interests to some extent, he soon complained that such strenuous, street-by-street explorations were too tiring and joined the group less and less frequently. As a native New Yorker there was little of the city that Kleiner had failed to explore in his thirty-five years, and revisiting completely familiar squares and historic byways had no very strong appeal for him. I was just a little less familiar with every between-building lane and seldom-visited churchyard in the city of my birth. But just the fact that I had college classes to attend on the following day prevented me from participating in those nighttime jaunts as often as I would have liked.

CHAPTER FOURTEEN

There undoubtedly were several reasons for the collapse of HPL's marriage. In her own account Sonia has discussed two or three fairly obvious ones which are common to almost all marriages, successful or otherwise. Just to what extent sexual incompatibility entered into the relationship, one can only speculate. It was something HPL never discussed with me; his ingrained puritanism was too pronounced and it would have gone contrary to what he felt should be the code of a gentleman.

I never doubted that Sonia was the very opposite of a cold and unresponsive woman in the realm of Eros, despite her own puritanism, and would ordinarily have expected a great deal of a man in a love relationship. But in Howard's case I think she would also have been capable of making allowance for his lack of romantic ardor, for she was genuinely and quite deeply in love with him. That he was lacking in such ardor hardly needs to be elaborated upon, for in his correspondence, with me and with others, the way he felt about sex was extremely self-revealing.

I have always believed, although it goes contrary to the Freudian hypothesis and psychoanalytic theory in general, that there are a few men of tremendous creative energies who are so lacking in erotic sensuality that sex does not have the importance for them that it does for the overwhelming majority of men and women.

Emerson comes to mind almost immediately, and so do two or three other American writers, for whom Puritanism undoubtedly exerted considerable influence but who would probably have been much the same if they had not been exposed to that kind of childhood conditioning. Although undoubtedly accentuated by inhibitory factors, the problem seems much more physiologically basic. One has only to read Bernard Shaw's letters to Frank Harris to be made aware that sex was very far from his major preoccupation, or even that it ever meant a great deal to him, despite the fact that in his later years he once boasted that "If I ever ate meat, no woman in London would be safe."

I do not in any case believe that it was sexual disharmony which led to the disintegration of the marriage. It was chiefly the economic factor which recent studies have established beyond dispute is responsible for four-fifths of all marital failures. If Howard had been under no economic strain it may well have been what is often referred to, even today, as a "good marriage." They were congenial in many ways; and while Howard would never have permitted a woman to dominate him to any major extent, he was so much the opposite of a male chauvinist that I doubt whether he would be regarded with hostile eyes today if he walked into a gathering of "Women's Lib" extremists and dwelt at length as a guest speaker on how he felt about marriage.

He realized that marriage involves on the part of both partners the making of many concessions. He knew that in small matters it is illogical—as well as time-wasting—for a man to resent every small episode in which a woman may seem, to an outsider unfamiliar with the entire relationship, to be "wearing the pants."

And I think he was discerning enough to realize as well that women, in the main, do not fall in love with men because of their strengths, but because of their weaknesses, and that if a man conceals his strengths to some extent, he is ten times as likely to arouse something in a woman which will defend him to the death against any kind of calumny. That is, perhaps, a slightly self-serving consideration, but it is one that can contribute substantially to the success of a marriage.

Howard's knowledge that his marriage was becoming increasingly threatened, but might still be preserved if he could somehow manage to gain more financial security (a possibility that seemed to him remote), kept him inwardly tormented during his last few months in New York. Every time I saw him, I was shocked by the change in his appearance. He had lost considerable weight and had the haggard look of a man who had passed sleepless nights haunted by an impasse which he was powerless to resolve.

It was not, of course, his marriage alone—it was the feeling that he could no longer endure living in New York. His disillusionment with the city had become so pronounced that he dreaded returning to the Clinton Street rooming house for fear that the people he passed on the street would pose a threat to his sanity, merely by what to him had become an intolerable, almost sinister sense of alienage. My mother quickly realized that his sanity might indeed be imperiled if another month passed without a prospect of rescue and wrote a long letter to his aunts, describing the situation in detail. I doubt whether Sonia even knew about that letter. At least she never mentioned it in recalling that particular period. Two days later a letter from Mrs. Clark arrived at the Brooklyn rooming house in the morning mail, accompanied by a railway ticket and a small check.

Very shortly—I am not certain, but I seem to recall it was not more than ten days later at most—Howard was on a train bound for Providence, after bidding goodbye to me at the station.

Our first visit to the Poe cottage in the Bronx in the company of Morton has been described elsewhere. But Howard and I visited the cottage a second time a fortnight before he returned to Providence; later we sat for perhaps an hour on the embankment adjacent to High Bridge where Poe often walked, discussing not only Poe but the stately mansion on the Manhattan side of the bridge where Washington, a frequent guest, probably spent more than one sleepless night.

Standing in front of the cottage for the second time, I recalled something I had once read about Poe's Fordham years. He had, it seems, made an appointment with a Manhattan editor which was of great importance to him, but had been prevented from keeping it by the most pitiful of accidents—a broken shoelace and not even sufficient money to purchase a new one!

After the lapse of a century and a quarter, such tragedies become so historically remote that they lose their aspect of immediacy, and it is easy to forget that the incident actually happened to a living, flesh-and-blood Poe standing, just as we were, in the shadow of the cottage. To him it was *very real,* and could hardly have failed to have been accompanied by a feeling of total wretchedness and despair.

A little of that realness becomes lost with the passage of time. But I have always believed that when such incidents bear directly on the daily lives of men and women of genius, they become—or should become—different from the way we would ordinarily be expected to feel about past cataclysmic events which have adorned the pages of history at swiftly recurring intervals.

What made this incident particularly outrageous was the simple fact that Poe was not unknown to fame at the time, having written *The Raven* a short while previously and having become as much discussed as Longfellow or any other poet of that era. He had even angered Longfellow at a much earlier period because of the harshness of his criticism, and evoked the kind of response that would have been meaningless if Poe had been less widely known.

HPL's virtually desperate economic situation at the time, and the impending termination of a marriage in which that factor played so large a role, made Poe's plight in the last years of his life seem a not too dissimilar kind of tragedy. It was made less tragic by the fact that Howard had been spared Poe's most grievous affliction—the desperate illness of a young bride. And less outrageous because Howard had received such scanty recognition as a writer that there was no way his plight could have become widely known. He was also younger than Poe had been in that terrible, sere autumn when every falling leaf must have seemed to him the equivalent of a tolling bell. And economically HPL's situation was not quite so extreme.

But still—I decided to say nothing to him about the parallel which I had drawn.

CHAPTER FIFTEEN

In trying to convey an accurate impression of what Lovecraft was really like, I am going to assume that he is sitting in a chair facing me, and I shall ask him once again exactly how he felt about Providence, New York, the Kalem Club gatherings; about his many correspondents, particularly such fellow writers as Clark Ashton Smith, August Derleth, Donald Wandrei, and Robert E. Howard; and about the universe in general, exactly as I did so many times in the past. (That seems an inordinately long sentence, but since Henry James often ran a sentence to two full pages and Faulkner to well over two hundred words, I have decided to let it stand, since it has been sanctioned by such illustrious exemplars!)

I have discussed in another chapter the changes which have taken place in American life and in the world itself since Howard's passing, in relation to how I believe he would have responded to them. But there is no need to speculate on how he felt about the national or international scene before 1937, for he left no stone unturned in the realm of totally candid appraisals to make that unambiguous. His conversations with me were always detailed and memorable whenever he touched upon matters of vital concern for him.

It is difficult to know where to begin, since so many things were discussed each time I met him in the fifteen years of our friendship. Howard was seldom silent for more than three or four minutes, for although, like everyone else, he could occasionally find that he had exhausted one subject and just the slightest trace of boredom could prevent him from approaching another with quite the same unfaltering zest and enthusiasm, he possessed an amazing capacity for recharging his verbal batteries. Actually they recharged themselves automatically and he never had to worry about slowing down in an awkward, slightly embarrassing manner in talking with anyone.

His answers to several of the questions which curiosity had prompted me to ask were as lengthy as they would have been if he had responded in a hundred page letter. But since none of his replies were notable for brevity, I may as well start with one of the longest ones, since they will all have to be abbreviated substantially, and I can think of no more important subject than how he had always felt about the city of his birth.

It is equally important to bear in mind that he has now returned to the chair he so often occupied, and that I am asking him the questions as if for the first time:

FBL: I've never doubted that Providence is the equal of any eastern city in scenic attractiveness and that it is associated in your mind with the New England past in the closest possible way. So New York would have to seem alien to you to a very great extent, and Boston or Salem or Portsmouth less alien, of course. But still you've often said that permanent residence in any other city would make you feel so uprooted that you would be totally miserable if you had to live anywhere else. Isn't that misery, that wretchedness, just a little neurotic? I mean, after all—

HPL: You may call it neurotic if you wish. After an old gentleman reaches a certain age, you can't separate him from his natural acres—the vistas he has always most cherished and which he has inherited from ancestors who felt as he did—without making him feel uprooted. Why should I pretend to be the kind of person I'm not, or could ever force myself to become? Providence will always be the only city that gives me the feeling that I am at home, in harmony with every aspect of the streets and surrounding countryside—a part of something I've known from birth and should never have left to spend two dreadful years in New York. No matter how often I may make brief trips to Charleston and New Orleans and Quebec, I shall never reside anywhere else. It is in Providence that the old gentleman will be buried. God Save the King, and his Colony of Rhode-Island and Providence-Plantations!

FBL: but you felt quite differently during your first few months in New York. You went into ecstasies over all of the colonial period architecture—street after street of old houses, the sunset traceries against the sky in Prospect Park, the skyline when you viewed it from Loveman's apartment in Brooklyn Heights. Have you forgotten all that? And "the gang," the walks you took—and the museum visits. Meeting and talking with me so often may have put a slight damper on your high spirits, since there has always been a twentieth century side to my personality which made the eighteenth century recede a little. But even so—

HPL: You know better than that. The Kalem Club helped more than anything else to make those first few months endurable. But it all changed for me very quickly. The crowds, the strange faces, the malevolence closing in, the hideous slums, particularly in the Red Hook section and in parts of Manhattan—well, I don't have to remind you how I felt when I saw the ancient spires and steeples of Providence looming up again from a train window.

FBL: But there are slums in Providence. Some rather depressing ones, I imagine, although I haven't seen them and you've never talked about them or described them in your letters.

HPL: The slums you've known from childhood are never quite so ugly or they don't seem so ugly. They always depressed me. Slums seem horrible and unnatural and one wishes they did not have to exist. I'm sure Dr. Johnson felt the same way about the infinitely more hideous slums of London.

FBL: Don't you know?

HPL: Oh, yes—he mentioned the horror in some of his talks with Boswell. And no doubt he avoided them in his walks as much as possible. (*I cannot vouch for Howard's very strict adherence to the truth here, for it has been many years since I have dipped into the most famous of all precedent-shattering biographies, though I have read five or six of the huge volumes of Boswellian letters that were published about twenty years ago. What fascinated me most about Boswell's biography of Johnson when I first read it at fifteen were the odd little neurotic quirks which he ascribed to Johnson, such as stopping in his walks to count every other cobblestone, or the way he chided Boswell occasionally for his amorousness, which as Boswell made plain in his Tour of the Hebrides, was just as pronounced in Johnson—even more so, perhaps, but more hypocritically concealed beneath layers of pretense.*)

FBL: Bob Howard seems to have felt much the same way about Texas as you do about Providence. There is no evidence in any of the very long letters he wrote to you that he was at odds with his environment. But Texas was quite different from Rhode Island. Doesn't it seem a little strange that a writer of imaginative fiction in the domain of fantasy could have been so completely at home in perhaps the most rugged environment in America? He seems to have had a very pronounced "lonely dreamer" side to his nature. He was extremely sensitive to poetic nuances, even if that sensitivity never enabled him even to approach, on a serious literary level, what Clark Ashton Smith achieved in his poems and stories.

HPL: It wasn't in the least strange. He was "Two-Gun Bob" in most of his stories, a sturdy adventurer who could identify with Conan so completely that it's difficult to think of them as separate individuals. The background of the Conan stories may have been mythical, but it was very like Texas in its major features. A rude, somewhat primitive early world antedating the pyramids, barbaric and colorful and imaginatively splendid in its total lack of literary artifice.

FBL: To me "Two-Gun Bob" has always seemed far from an important writer, except perhaps in one rather unusual respect. He had all of the tremendous zest, of adventurous delight in fictional encounters on the heroic level that we associate with the novels of Jack London. But he remains, I feel, predominantly a writer for boys. And he died too young to have become as accomplished as London in that particular realm. He might have surpassed London as a craftsman if he had gone on, however, and fulfilled his youthful promise. Do you agree with that appraisal?

HPL: To a considerable extent, I do. But, as you've just pointed out, he could weave the kind of magical spell that Jack London would have been incapable of weaving—the kind of spell that proves, beyond any possibility of doubt, that he had something in common with both Smith and Dunsany. There are dream pinnacles in the Conan stories that are remote from the kind of novels that made Jack London famous. There is no mingling of the immediate and the elusively dreamlike, the mythical and the fabulous in *The Sea Wolf* or *The Call of the Wild*. (*I could not ask HPL what he thought of the school of "Sword & Sorcery" tenting in general, which Bob Howard had undoubtedly been among the first to make popular, because the term had not been coined before 1937. August Derleth wrote me, in one of his last letters, that he felt that Fritz Leiber excelled all other living authors in that particular genre.*)

FBL: Naturally Bob Howard and Jack London did not always deal with the same kind of fictional material. And pure fantasy was not London's forte at all, although *The Iron Heel* is a kind of utopian fantasy not so different from Bellamy's *Looking Backward*, apart from its socialistic orientation. But I was thinking of something a little different. London was the kind of writer who could instill in his readers a lively awareness of what it means to be very young, eager and strong and confident, and hell-bent for "red-blooded adventure." That's a trite, rather silly term, but it pretty well covers it. And Bob Howard was like that, too, in a way. Remember, he wrote many sport stories, western tales, straight adventure yarns. He was even, in some respects, what today would be called a "gut" writer. Not an adult, realistic gut writer exactly, but the kind that appeals to youth. (*I almost said, "that accounts, in a large measure, for his tremendous popularity among the young today," quite forgetting that "today" would have meant 1937 for HPL at the latest.*) What I'm really trying to say is that he was the kind of writer who might well have been remembered for all of the qualities which made Jack London famous. London's fame has dwindled but he remains far from forgotten today, and Bob Howard might well have surpassed him as a writer of adventure fiction par excellence. Do you agree?

HPL: Yes, I've no quarrel with you as to that. But his passing at so early an age was a tragedy that has been many times repeated. One has to be grateful for what he did accomplish.

FBL: Incidentally, I was sixteen when I first read *The Sea Wolf*, and this book changed the summer for me. We were vacationing in the Thousand Islands, and it wasn't the St. Lawrence that went sweeping past the Inn on the Canadian shore. It was the open sea, and that hell ship stayed in view for days. I suppose it wouldn't be considered a serious novel from a literary point of view, but it has something. That's what I meant when I compared Bob Howard to London—they both had the same kind of gusto—an unspoiled kind of something that you don't find in too many writers. What do you think of Jack London? I've never asked you.

HPL: It's not the kind of writing that could have a very strong appeal for an old gentleman, I'm afraid. I've always been too land-based to feel very strongly drawn to the sea. (*It has been said that Howard hated the sea, but that was not at all true; it was only seafood that he could not abide. He liked the sea, despite what he may have said in some of his letters. I even think he felt much the same way about it as did most of the English poets, but it amused him to pretend otherwise.*) But you're right about London. He was just a widely read popular novelist, but *The Sea Wolf* had a certain Nietzschean, "ruthless superman" fascination about it. It depicted the brutal sadist at his worst, a warped and repellent figure, but a figure made peculiarly unusual by the fact that he was the opposite of unread and uncultivated in one aspect of his personality. London was the first American writer to put a sensitive and imaginative man of letters in direct confrontation with that kind of human monster, on the quarterdeck of a ship, at least, where Wolf Larsen was in a position to exercise absolute tyranny. That was unusual enough as an historical foreshadowing in the fiction of the 1910 period to entitle London, I've always believed, to a small measure of literary permanence.

FBL: "Literary permanence" is about the highest tribute that can be paid a writer. Do you think any member of our group will ever attain it? None of us are even popular novelists or short story writers. We'd have a very long road to travel to get as far as that. And if we crashed the *Saturday Evening Post* or *Collier's*—a distinct possibility, of course—we'd still be a considerable distance from the more serious kind of literary recognition that bears only the most tenuous relationship to the slicks in general. Even two or three stories in *Harper's* or *The Atlantic Monthly* or *The Dial* wouldn't mean very much.

HPL: That would depend upon the quality of our stories, not in what magazine we crashed or failed to crash. If our stories were of literary quality, the chances are they could all be published in the *Police Gazette* and eventually they would be singled out and preserved.

FBL: After how long a time? Fifty years?

HPL: You've got to remember, for one thing, that there is no wide market for supernatural horror stories in America today. It's tragic, but we have to face it. In England it's a little different, but there's only a very small readership for the novels of Machen, Blackwood, Walter de la Mare, M. P. Shiel, and M. R. James on this side of the Atlantic. Our best bet still resides in the hardcover book field, however, and probably always will. August is far ahead of the rest of us because he had the good sense to make the writing of supernatural horror stories an avocation. He did what he most wanted to do by writing regional novels. And because he is a splendid writer who will go even further than he has, he may well be assured of literary permanence. But the rest of us are far less versatile—although you've at least branched out into other fields. The old gentleman could never have written and sold forty or fifty science fiction stories. (*Until about 1935— and I am assuming that Howard is occupying the chair opposite me on one of his frequent visits to New York around that time—l had sold science fiction short stories to most of the "scientifiction" pulp magazines, and very "pulpish" most of them were. Later when the so-called "new" science fiction developed in conjunction with the appearance of John W. Campbell as editor of* Astounding Science Fiction *and* Unknown, *I wrote about thirty stories—ten or twelve of them have been included in my Arkham House volumes—which l prefer, with perhaps four exceptions, to all of my early work for* Weird Tales.) The kind of literary permanence—"survival" might be a better term—you've just been talking about is an uncertain thing at best. How can anyone really know? A writer of genius could be totally forgotten, if an early magazine containing his best work happened to have been published by some obscure, careless young printer who forgot to set aside a few copies wrapped in cellophane.

FBL: But at least a few of the early issues of Weird Tales will not share that fate. When sixty thousand copies of a magazine are in print they can't all be lost, no matter how yellow and brittle the pages may become.

HPL: No, but they can be so few in number that no one would take the trouble to search around for a copy without some immediate and compelling need to do so. And that need would not even arise if a writer failed to become widely known through his later work.

FBL: But Clark Ashton Smith and Donald Wandrei are very much alive and will go on writing for other magazines. And they've each appeared in Weird Tales a number of times.

HPL: I know. I was just postulating an extreme example. I don't think Smith or Wandrei will be soon forgotten in the fantasy and weird fiction fields. Derleth has achieved recognition on a double, more firmly established basis, as I said a moment ago.

FBL: Do you think that CAS and Donald will be remembered in the years to come—thirty or fifty years from now?

HPL: Their work is distinguished by the sort of cosmic vision which has always made me feel that I could fully appreciate how the vastness of space, which reduces man to insignificance, must have impressed them from an early age. It has always impressed me in the same way, but in the work of few other writers have I found a genuine understanding of this. It is not present in your writing to any extent.

FBL: No, I'm afraid it isn't. I can understand it, of course. But it just doesn't rush in upon me and grip me in the same emotional way.

HPL: That's what I meant. August readily admits to the same limitation. It is certainly no disgrace, for Balzac, Thomas Hardy, and—yes, even H. G. Wells, despite his preoccupation with travel through time and space, didn't seem to experience emotions similar to mine when he contemplated the stellar immensities which make the solar system seem like a grain of dust.

CHAPTER SIXTEEN

My first, quite early visit to Providence was almost coincidental with HPL's return to his native city, for it occurred not more than ten or twelve months later. It was part of an itinerary which would take the entire Long family to Canada on a visit to both Montreal and Quebec, with stopovers at Saratoga Springs and Lake George on the return journey.

As soon as I informed Howard of the impending visit, I received by return mail a 20,000 word travelogue, detailing all the points of antiquarian interest we *must not miss* on the route we followed from the outskirts of the city to 10 Barnes Street. It has always been a source of deep regret to me that we could not have approached 10 Barnes on the Ancient Hill by so circuitous a route that every one of those sites could have been explored at leisure, even if it had delayed our arrival by three full days.

But that would have meant imposing a wholly unpardonable burden on my father, since, although I had a learner's driving permit at the time, I very seldom felt justified in taking the wheel for more than a few hours, on some road in the open countryside where innocent pedestrians would not have been imperiled. So we abandoned all thought of tarrying anywhere within the boundaries of the city and drove directly to 10 Barnes.

It is curious how little can be recalled sometimes about the outside aspect of a dwelling which one has visited for the first time as an invited guest, particularly when so much of interest keeps taking place indoors that no time remains for making architectural observations. We passed quickly into the house and our stay was brief; and even though on our departure the following morning I could have paused for a moment to look up at the house, I failed to do so. I do not believe it was just the passage of time that has blurred my impressions in that respect. It was just something that happened, so that until my second visit to Providence several years later I had no clear picture whatsoever of the Barnes Street residence as it looked from the street. I just pictured it as a house—any frame house of attractive appearance on a tree-lined street, without distinguishing characteristics.

But indoors it was quite different. There was a very small room opposite the front door which Mrs. Clark, Howard's older aunt, had arranged in advance, and as soon as my parents had been conducted to a larger room on the ground floor she returned to set it in order again—fussing over everything until she felt it would be exactly the kind of room that would provide a maximum of overnight comfort for Belknapius, about whom she had heard so much.

She was a very tiny woman, and there was about her an aura of kindliness and gentility—the genuine, Down East kind of gentility that had nothing in common with the slight suggestion of snobbish pride and reserve that such an adjective sometimes conveys.

After she departed I had taken a pair of pajamas from my overnight bag, draped them over the foot of the bed, and placed on the chiffonier a hairbrush, tube of toothpaste, and a pipe, when I heard voices at the end of the long hall. I decided that the time had come to greet Howard in the study where he often wrote far into the night, with the shades drawn to shut out even a glimmer of light from the street. The voices indicated that he was not alone, but I had not the remotest idea who the visitor, or visitors, might be.

When I had walked to the end of the hall and turned right, I found out quickly enough; for there emerged from the room the tall, slightly stooped form of C. M. Eddy, whose story, *The Loved Dead,* Howard had partly revised and one perhaps might say had ghost-written. (It was this story which greatly increased the circulation of *Weird Tales* during a period of financial crisis by virtually getting the magazine banned.) Eddy did not look in the least like a ghoul, although at the time he was just a little on the gaunt side.

When he saw me he instantly extended his hand and gestured me into the study. His handclasp was quite firm, but with no hint of the boniness that one customarily associates with every variety of tomb-dweller.

"Welcome, Belknapius," he said, in the opposite of a sepulchral voice and without preamble, as if he were greeting an old acquaintance from the gulfs between the stars and had no need to introduce himself.

The instant Howard saw me hovering in the doorway he smiled broadly, arose from his desk in a far corner of the room, and advanced toward me in three long strides.

"Mrs. Clark wouldn't let me emerge from this room until you'd had an opportunity to find out for yourself what pleasant provisions for making a guest feel at home a Providence mausoleum can provide," he said. "If you haven't had dinner—"

"That's taken care of," I said. "We stopped at a lunch wagon about two hours ago. We may as well just sit around and talk. I doubt if we'll run out of conversation for some time."

"We've been talking for three hours," Howard said. "But the whole night is before us. If your parents would like to join us—"

"They're quite tired," I said. "My father especially. He did almost all of the driving."

"Belknapius doesn't like to drive a car," he told Eddy. "I can't even imagine how I'd feel at the wheel of a car. I'm glad I'll never be compelled to run over anyone."

"I haven't done that so far—not even a cat."

"Oh, don't—please," Howard protested. "That would be terrible."

"You'd feel just as bad if it were an old man on crutches."

"Well, maybe *almost* as bad. But a *cat*—"

The three-way conversation which ensued lasted until long past midnight. Eddy was a free-lance writer interested in making as many story sales as possible, and his circumstances were such that he was forced to consider only the more commercial aspects of authorship. Howard understood that necessity and made no attempt to discourage him by stressing that even if a writer gave no thought to anything but the mechanics of popular magazine writing, it was often very difficult to sell stories to editors whose sole criterion in judging a submission was whether or not it would increase or diminish the magazine's circulation.

We spoke of other things as well, and ended by discussing T. S. Eliot and *The Wasteland* which had only recently appeared in *The Dial*. Howard could see nothing about it that was deserving of permanence: "A passing fad, a disorganized kind of decadence." But, surprisingly enough, Eddy at least to some extent shared my admiration for it. (I had previously read, at Alfred Galpin's urging, Eliot's first book of poems, *The Sacred Wood,* at the Forty-second Street Library and had walked out of the reading room that afternoon with the feeling that something new had indeed been added, and that American poetry would never be quite the same again. It has not been, but so many years have passed since *The Wasteland* appeared in *The Dial* that it seems today very much a kind of classical museum piece.)

The following morning *my* aunt arrived in Providence and we met her for breakfast at the Crown Hotel; I ordered, I remember, a hard-boiled egg which arrived soft, and although I would have shrugged it off as of no great importance, my aunt became indignant and ordered the waiter to reboil it. My aunt then became a fourth passenger in the Long family car, and we drove to Quebec—a city which HPL had not yet visited but would later describe in a hundred page travelogue—and returned to New York ten days later.

During the next seven or eight years my visits to Providence were almost as short in duration as that very early trip, and we met more often by bus or train in other parts of New England. On one of the earlier visits, however, I remained long enough to accompany him on a guided tour of the city, very similar to the antiquarian jaunts in the early New York days on which he had been so enthusiastic an explorer of ivy-walled courtyards and churchyard burial plots hidden from the gaze of the unobservant. During that Providence tour he may well have paused before the "Shunned House" on Benefit Street, but I have no recollection of him having done so. Several years earlier he had written the story which was to confer upon this dwelling the terrifying uniqueness that sets it apart from every other structure—nighted tomb or crumbling mortuary crypt or Innsmouth-located fisherman's shack—in the "Collected Works of H. P. Lovecraft, Gent." But what made that tour so totally memorable were the moments when he came to an abrupt halt before every cypress-shadowed graveyard or gambrel-roofed house or time-eroded curbstone in parts of the city where Poe once walked when he was courting Mrs. Whitman. Here Howard paused, and spoke with reverent accompanying gestures.

On my last visit to Providence he was living at 66 College Street and was quite startled when I arrived at the door and sounded the antique bronze knocker in the company of a young lady he had never met, and who had come from California on a visit. But I doubt if there were another young lady in America at the time it would have given him more pleasure to meet, because she had talked with Clark Ashton Smith. She lived in Auburn, had known Smith quite well from childhood, and her name was Helen V. Sully.

Sixty-six College Street had a two-level living room and we spent the entire afternoon on the upper portion discussing the "ghoul-haunted woodlands" of Auburn and Clark Ashton Smith's poems and stories and incredible sculptured figurines fashioned in the image of one or more of the Old Ones.

There was one previous visit which involved an incident that seems, in some strange way, to be too prophetic to be coincidental. Some years after HPL's earliest stories had appeared in *Weird Tales,* we were walking along an elm-shaded street on the Ancient Hill when he showed me an early letter from Robert Bloch which he had just received, accompanied by a macabre drawing.

"This is from a sixteen year old correspondent," he told me. "He saw one of my *Weird Tales* stories and has written to me at length several times. He both draws and writes, and I can't decide whether his stories or his artwork show the greater promise. But I can tell you this. The kid is brilliant. He'll go very far—perhaps as far as Clark Ashton Smith. Just look at this—it's really quite tremendous."

That is one of those predictions which have about them an aura of the uncanny, and I have never forgotten it. In some ways it seems inextricably tied in with Jung's theory of synchronicity which does not exclude clairvoyant extensions of a parallel kind of relation between two events which are at variance with the laws of causality. Or with Dunne's extraordinary speculation about the time stream, which H. G. Wells admired and seems to have taken seriously. Dunne believed that we quite possibly return and relive our lives over and over, with a few minor variations each time. The entire pattern becomes a matter of record, encapsulated in Space and Time, and at any point in that record a particular moment in time could be removed and synchronized with some later moment by an unusual flash of precognitive clairvoyance in the course of a casual discussion.

If that younger Robert Bloch is still very much in existence, as Dunne's surmise implies, the Bloch of today could have been just as much in existence clairvoyantly in the depths of HPL's mind when that astounding prediction was made. I am certain Howard would have refused to believe this, and I place very little credence in it myself, but it is a fascinating surmise notwithstanding.

A few years later during one of Howard's return visits to New York, I introduced him to L. Ron Hubbard, long before Hubbard became the founder of Scientology. Many of my stories appeared later in *Astounding Science Fiction* and *Unknown* in issues containing the stories which Hubbard also wrote for John W. Campbell, but that, too, was quite a few years in the future.

At that time Hubbard was very young, and a member of an early writers' group presided over by Arthur J. Burks which met each month at a midtown restaurant. Hubbard was not an inconspicuous presence on such occasions; in those years he had bright red hair, and at five minute intervals during the course of these gatherings he would remove from his pocket a cigarette lighter attached to a long chain, for he apparently was a compulsive smoker who could empty two packages of cigarettes with incredible rapidity.

Later I met and talked with Hubbard perhaps a dozen times at the home of Malcolm Jameson (also an early contributor to *Astounding Science Fiction*), but at that time I had exchanged no more than a few words with him. I felt the brief exchange justified my introducing him to Howard, since they occupied adjoining seats at the table, and the two engaged in quite a long conversation.

"That red-headed young man is *most* extraordinary," was HPL's comment, when we left the restaurant at the termination of the gathering.

That comment also seems to have assumed an aspect of the precognitively clairvoyant.

CHAPTER SEVENTEEN

Howard always insisted that he did not believe in supernatural occurrences of any kind; ghosts in the traditional sense he attributed to superstitious credulity on a childishly primitive level. On one occasion I decided to put his skepticism to the test.

I conjured up a ghost. I did not resort to trickery, however. I merely took advantage of the environment in which our discussion took place. It was the kind of environment which would have made the materialization of a spectral presence seem almost as inevitable as it would have been had we been raised high into the air by a sudden gust of wind, blowing cold upon us and shattering every attic window in a house reputed to be haunted.

The discussion took place during a visit to Newburyport. We had spent the afternoon on the sunlit porch of a local resident, a New Englander of the old school whose grandparents had been influenced by the wave of occultism which swept New England a century ago and resulted in the founding of an occult-oriented religious sect. Our host did not himself place much credence in the occult, but having read several of Howard's stories he was eager to recommend a brief visit to an historic graveyard where "hauntings" were rumored to be almost nightly in occurrence.

HPL was interested, of course. But only because ancient graveyards were as fascinating to him as the moldering crypts he liked to think could be found far beneath the pews of certain steepled New England churches, if one conducted a diligent enough search.

We waited for the coming of dusk, and then set out, unaccompanied by our host, through a number of narrow, seaward-sloping lanes, with gambrel-roofed houses casting long shadows on the uneven paving stones as we progressed.

Fifteen minutes later we were seated in the graveyard, on a grass-covered burial mound with a crumbling tombstone at its head. The inscription on the weathered stone might well have read: "As I am now, you will someday be," since inscriptions of a somewhat similar nature were common enough in New England graveyards two centuries ago. (We seem to have lost the grim sense of funereal humor which could cast a pall on the living without diminishing the joy that goes just with being alive!)

Unfortunately a respect for absolute veracity compels me to add that the tombstone contained no such inscription. It bore only a name and a date.

But even so, no setting could have been more spectrally evocative, for a heavy fog which had begun to drift in from the sea was assuming a nebulously weaving, highly suggestive effect. "Howard, there's something I've always been curious about," I told him. "Suppose you were seated on a grave like this—not necessarily this particular grave—and a shape rose up out of the mound that you couldn't possibly mistake for anything but a ghost. Let's say it just hovered above the grave for a moment as a very attenuated spiral of mist, in vaguely human form. But it didn't stay attenuated. It coalesced into a very firm-looking specter, with every lineament sharply defined and with eyes like holes in a skull. Would you doubt its genuineness and fail to be badly shaken?"

It took Howard barely a second to reply. "Shaken? Of course not."

"But what would you think? How could you hope to explain it?"

It had occurred to me that he might take refuge in the usual commonplace explanation. Visual hallucinations occur more frequently than is commonly supposed. Extreme nervous tension or any unusual strain can produce them, even though they are more often associated with severe mental illness. But I doubted if that explanation would have been acceptable to HPL, and I was not mistaken.

"There would be many ways of accounting for it," he said. "And they would have nothing to do with my emotional state at the time."

"Many ways? Apart from a supernatural explanation, I can't think of one."

"It would, of course, be difficult to explain," Howard conceded. "But that's beside the point. I'd know instantly, beyond the remotest possibility of doubt, that it couldn't be a ghost. So I'd start searching about in my mind for some other explanation. I can think of several that would not stretch credulity one-tenth as far as a surrender to blind superstition."

"Name one."

"If someone suggested a visit to the graveyard in question, I would consider him a highly probable suspect. I would take very seriously the possibility that he'd planned it in advance of my arrival, as a skillfully contrived hoax."

"You must have taken that brief talk you once had with Houdini with the utmost seriousness, despite what you told me at the time—that you found it more superficially amusing than otherwise," I said. "Do you actually believe even Houdini could have made a wisp of mist arise from a grave and take on form and substance right before your eyes? Quietly, unobtrusively, with no more than a slight rustling sound?"

"The illustration you cite is illogical to begin with," Howard countered. "You're implying such an occurrence *could* take place. But that's merely an assumption on your part. I won't argue with you about that aspect of it, however. No matter how much you may add to it as you go along, I can assure you that apparent supernatural manifestations are always illusory. There always has to be some entirely logical explanation for everything that appears to contradict what a truly sensible person should have made up his mind about from the age of six on the basis of simple observation. I realized, even earlier than that, that there's a stability about nature in all of its manifestations that nothing can alter, outside of some cataclysm that is itself the opposite of supernatural."

"As to that—our views are identical," I told him. "But even if I'm talking about an occurrence that's hard to imagine as taking place—*what if it did?* It's just how you'd *feel* if it did that I'm interested in."

"Well, I've told you. I probably picked out a needlessly complicated explanation. There are a few simpler ones. Some local prankster—"

"I know what you're going to say. Someone imbecilic might be flashing a projected image from a distance that could be controlled in an illusion-creating way."

"It would certainly occur to me," Howard said, with a very slight overtone of satisfaction in his voice.

"But suppose the shape was just too close and too real. Suppose you could detect the foetid odor of its breath? Suppose it reached out and grabbed hold of you?"

"It still wouldn't shake my conviction that ghosts are an absolute absurdity and there would have to be some other way of explaining it."

HPL noticed it before I did. Four graves away, one of the fog wisps from the sea had spiraled upward on a mound where fallen twigs and the shriveled leaves of more than one autumn had accumulated to an unusual extent, giving it so neglected a look that it appeared to be a grave less visited than the ones surrounding it, ancient as all of them were.

Less visited because it had been deliberately shunned? The thought would not have entered my mind if the rising spiral of mist had not taken on so close a resemblance to a human form. There were two arms and a head; and although the arms were of uneven length and one trailed off in a long streamer of wavering mist, that very fact was more in accord with a spectral apparition than otherwise.

I knew, of course, that it could not possibly be anything of the sort. It was not even particularly unusual, since if one enters any ancient graveyard at dusk filled with mists blowing in from the sea, there would likely be more than one such shape. The human form is far less complicated in outward structure than that of a spider crab or a giraffe, and floating ribbons of mist have a tendency to collect in one place and assume just such an appearance. But still—I knew that Howard was aware of what had taken place, because I heard him chuckling softly to himself. Before I could turn to stare at him, he gripped my wrist and pointed.

"Look over there," he said. "There's your ghost. Would you expect me to be startled by that?"

"No," I said. "I guess not. It isn't remotely comparable in ghostliness to the witches we saw in a twilight glow in Inwood about six years ago."

"You mean, at the Cloisters? Well—I'll have to confess that did shake me up a little for a moment."

The "witches" were far less coincidental in occurrence, because their appearance had not been preceded by any reference to the supernatural. We had just emerged from the subway after a ride from Brooklyn to the wide stretch of woodland at the northern tip of Manhattan (a ride calculated to make anyone, particularly HPL, understand precisely what Henry James meant when he called New York "that long city"), and our thoughts were not on ghosts at all. We were both extremely tired, and although we were accompanied by the indefatigable James F. Morton, whose energy always awed Howard, he likewise seemed rather uncommunicative, even a little depressed.

The Bernard Cloisters was a miracle of reconstruction, assembled by the sculptor whose name it bore, and transported from France brick by brick. Before he presented it as a gift to the Metropolitan Museum of Art, it occupied half an acre on his private estate in Inwood.

It was just as impressive as any similar shrine in Europe, with goblin tapestries and illuminated manuscripts vying in interior splendor with wood-carved figures, gilded or unadorned, dating back to the Middle Ages. For the most part the figures were angelic in aspect, but a few were chillingly demoniac with gargoyled features. It was easy to imagine a witches' brew concealed somewhere in the wings, sending up wisps of sulfurous vapor, if only because the Middle Ages could not do without something of that nature to give depth and meaning to its struggles with the "Powers of Darkness."

At that time the Cloisters was in the depths of a heavily forested region, and as we approached over a narrow, winding footpath we were instantly struck by the long and chilling shadows which the trees were casting in the deepening dusk.

Then we saw—the witches. Three bent and fragile-looking women, unmistakably well advanced in years, were sweeping up the fallen leaves surrounding the Cloisters with long-handled brooms. There was a twilight glimmer at their backs, and they were wearing what at least from a distance looked like jet-black, conically tapering hats.

It was the sort of scene to which no master of descriptive prose could possibly have done justice. For some inexplicable reason the twilight glow alone imparted an eerie unreality. Yet paradoxically it also seemed too frighteningly real for sanity to countenance.

It made such an unexpected, totally startling impression on me that to this day I can bring back the memory of it with the kind of total recall that verges upon the miraculous. I can still hear the crunch of the leaves underfoot, and the murmur of the wind in the branches overhead.

I am quite certain that Howard shared my startlement because it was the kind of scene that could turn him retrospectively ecstatic.

But if Morton had not come so abruptly to a halt and made it impossible for him outwardly to ignore the descent of three witches on broomsticks on Manhattan Island in the third decade of the twentieth century, I rather suspect he would have continued along the footpath without saying a word. So deep-seated was his disbelief in the supernatural that had he appeared to be even slightly shaken, his integrity in that respect would have been struck a grievous blow.

"Did you ever see anything so unheard of?" I can remember Morton asking. "The Cloisters, the deep woods—the woods alone couldn't look more like the kind of locality a coven would consider just right for a secret gathering at nightfall. It's as if those three crones were engaged in clearing away some of the underbrush in preparation for a sabbat."

"In all probability they are engaged in tidying up about the estate," Howard said. "Bernard's a wealthy man, and could easily spare that many domestics for a short while, to clear away an unusually heavy accumulation of fallen leaves. In early November—"

"We can find out quickly enough," Morton said, before he could go on. "Stay right here. I'm going to ask them why they feel they could accomplish that better, looking so much like witches. It could hardly have been staged for our benefit, since we're not here as individually invited guests."

That was true, of course. Bernard had graciously invited the public to visit the Cloisters free of charge, which elevated him to the stature of a splendidly dedicated sculptor in our eyes. But he could have had no idea that one of the early visitors would be HPL.

The witches were perhaps seventy or eighty feet from where we were standing, but Morton covered the distance in so swift and resolute a stride that he was engaging the nearest one in conversation before Howard could say anything more.

Ordinarily, I think, HPL would have been the first to confirm to his own satisfaction what he had just said. But talking to women to whom he had never been introduced went against his code as a gentleman, and their age was of no consequence, since he was so tactfully perceptive in that respect that he could easily imagine a woman of eighty-five feeling that she had as much right as a girl of eighteen to resent unauthorized "pickup" attempts by the amorously inclined.

Morton talked to only one of the witches, which suggested that he had secured from her all of the information which he needed to confirm or refute HPL's surmise.

"Well?" Howard asked, the instant Morton rejoined us with an amused look in his eyes.

"You guessed right," Morton said. "Or nearly right. One of them is a custodian of the illuminated manuscripts. The other two work about the place. They're wearing black cotton stocking on their heads as a protection against the dust. It hasn't rained for five days, so sweeping up the leaves is a dusty task. A makeshift turban like that looks very much like a witch hat tapering to a point."

"I thought of that immediately," Howard said. "Mrs. Gamwell"—Howard never called his aunts by their baptismal names—"wraps a wet cloth around her head when she has some dusting to do."

"How about the brooms?" I could not resist asking. "They seem long-handled enough to accommodate four or five witches, accompanied by one of their infernal black imps."

"I should think," I added, "they'd rake leaves with a hoe, or a wire-mesh broom."

"Belknapius has a slight tendency to raise objections about something that is perfectly uncomplicated on the face of it," Howard said, in the almost mischievously schoolboy tone of voice he occasionally adopted when in a humorously chiding mood. "Brooms can be of almost any length, and a long-handled one would be ideally suited to a task like that."

"After all," he added, with an irrelevant kind of levity that was not at all characteristic of him, "a broom is a broom is a broom is a broom."

Everyone at times makes inane remarks, of course, and it did not surprise me as much as it might have done had I not known how greatly he enjoyed parodying Swinburne and even Eliot and Pound. It was the first time, however, that he had ever parodied Gertrude Stein, for he had never mentioned her in all the talks I had had with him, and I had not known he was even familiar with "A rose is a rose is a rose...

Although the Cloisters did not restrict visitors to the formal closing hour schedule upon which museums insist, it was so late in the day that I doubted whether we would be allowed to remain in the Middle Ages for very long. But we were welcomed at the door, and spent an hour walking about inside, our footsteps echoing on the ancient stone floor very much as a Trappist's sandals might have done if they had been steel-soled.

Despite HPL's appreciation of the Gothic in literature, as evidenced by his thrice-reprinted essay, *Supernatural Horror in Literature,* the Middle Ages did not hold the fascination for him that it did for Morton and myself. And my fascination was not as great as perhaps it should have been, for a writer of horror stories. I could picture myself becoming wholly absorbed in the kind of journey into the past which the Cloisters provided for several hours, caught up in the strange, dark, brooding wonder and magnificence of the Middle Ages in the realm of architecture and statuary and illuminated manuscripts. But then I would have experienced an irresistible urge to walk out into the clear bright sunlight again, and with no lingering sense of regret, to let the heavy portals clang shut behind me.

But I have strayed quite far from where I left Howard before recalling to mind that visit to the Cloisters—sitting on a grave in an ancient Newburyport cemetery with a rising mist from the sea assuming a wraith like aspect above another grave a short distance away. Our conversation had carried us both quite far from the cemetery, but we did not arise and depart until another fifteen or twenty minutes had passed and the spectral shape had dissolved, giving Howard the triumphant feeling that he had won the argument we had been having from the start.

I was content to let him think that he had, because it really had not been an argument at all—just a testing. Basically I could not have agreed with him more. Actual spectral presences were for the birds.

CHAPTER EIGHTEEN

In the various panel discussions centering about HPL in which this writer has participated, I have particularly enjoyed answering the many questions hurled at me for the following reasons:

One—although I have never been able to overcome a certain shyness when I encounter people whose interests differ sharply from mine and who have little understanding of artists in general, I never seem to experience the same kind of self-consciousness on a lecture platform. Just why that is so I cannot say. It usually works in the opposite direction, and people who are completely relaxed and at ease socially are very likely to experience at least a slight touch of "stage fright." Even professional actors of long experience are occasionally thus afflicted.

Two—there is a casual give-and-take about lecture-panel questions which enables one to respond with a more rounded-out reply to some specific query than would be possible otherwise. The very nature of the question provides the kind of stimulation that taps the roots of memory on a most rewarding level.

Three—so many totally false assumptions, half-truths, and even malicious fabrications have circulated about HPL in the past decade that a systematic refutation becomes mandatory.

Before starting this chapter two alternatives were open to me. I could have presented some of the actual questions and my replies to them just as they occurred in the course of several panel discussions. Instead, I have decided to pose fifteen or twenty questions of my own choosing, differing in no important respect from the ones that were asked, but eliminating most of the inconsequential ramblings that no panel participant or solitary guest speaker can hope to avoid in the course of a lengthy discussion. With that established, let us begin:

Question: Just how eccentric was Lovecraft? Was he actually a kind of "oddball"? From some of the articles I've read about him, he must have behaved in a very peculiar way at times.

Answer: He was no more an "oddball," I'm sure, than Poe or

Shelley or Swinburne would have seemed if you could have met them in person. When Browning asked, "Did you once see Shelley plain?", he was thinking of the resplendence which must have emanated from so great a poet, as the image which Browning's reference in the same poem to a fallen eagle feather makes unmistakably clear. But if he could have traveled back in time and spoken with Shelley, he might well have been more aware of his several very pronounced eccentricities. Shelley was an "oddball" beyond any possibility of doubt, and no biographer has ever disputed that his behavior verged upon the extraordinary. Browning himself, incidentally, was also quite eccentric, and Oliver Goldsmith even more so.

No, HPL was no more of an "oddball" than a great many writers of genius. He had his eccentricities, of course, but not one of them could quite compete with the recorded peculiarities of three or four of the major figures in English or French literature, and a greater number of lesser figures. Samuel Johnson as depicted by Boswell comes instantly to mind, but Boswell himself was even more an "oddball"—perhaps, in sober actuality, the most wildly eccentric man of letters who ever walked the planet. Compared to the eccentricities of Boswell, HPL's fade into insignificance.

Question: But what of the seven or eight American writers who were established literary figures about forty-five years ago, during the period when Lovecraft was writing for *Weird Tales* and yet totally unknown otherwise? None of them had so many idiosyncrasies.

Answer: Don't be too sure. You didn't meet and talk with a single one of them, and thus are in exactly the same position that Browning was in relation to Shelley. Recent biographies of at least two of them reveal a pronounced "oddball" pattern of behavior once their character was fully explored. But I didn't intend to engage in so generalized a literary discussion. It's just that Lovecraft has so often been referred to as extremely eccentric, and I was forced to cite a few classic examples in refutation. I'm simply saying it was not Lovecraft's behavorial eccentricities that set him a little apart. It was something else entirely.

Question: What was it, then?

Answer: Like Blake, Coleridge, and Poe, Lovecraft was in thrall to the strange, the somber, the darkly terrifying, and the marvelous. That did set him apart and made him seem profoundly "different."

But the uniqueness which we associate with such writers does not even stem, in the main, from their comparative rareness as literary phenomena. It stems more from the fact that they contributed a new dimension to human experience by "dreaming dreams no mortal ever dared to dream before."

Question: All apart from his eccentricities which you feel were widely shared by other writers, and what you've just said about his writing, how do you explain the fact that he has been depicted as morbidly preoccupied with tombs and corpses and everything that is suggestive of decay, and the survival of hideous necrophilic entities from other dimensions of space and time? Wasn't that a neurotic aberration?

Answer: The preoccupation was evident enough, and he would have been the last to deny he had a bent for that kind of writing. But it had nothing to do with morbidity on a personal level, even though it amused him to create a contrary impression by picturing himself as a monster in first person narratives in which the tomb-dwelling character into whose shoes he had stepped would seem to many readers an autobiographical self-image.

Actually, he was no more of a monster than I am, despite the fact that I might experience a little difficulty in clearing myself of such a charge if I were to be confronted, in open court, by all of my published supernatural horror stories. In general, they follow more a "fire and sleet and candlelight" pattern than they do one of gruesome physical horror. But in a few of them death and postmortem disintegration are very much in evidence.

Question: But why so compulsive a need to create tomb-dwelling characters, when you don't run into them at all in everyday life?

Answer: Because it is the obligation of art to investigate everything that takes place in the dark of the human mind. And if you have a literary bent for supernatural horror or fantasy in general, the writing of such work makes you very happy. There's an inner joy to it, a sense of wonder and adventurous expectancy—to borrow one of Lovecraft's most frequently used terms. If you're lucky, you'll be able to write a poem or story that will depict what you've encountered in your explorations which will make others happy in the same secret, wholly miraculous way.

Lewis Carroll was very lucky in that respect—and so was Poe.

And I have no doubt at all that Lovecraft will be thought just as lucky in the years ahead.

Question: It is happening now, isn't it?

Answer: Yes, it is happening today. Whether in another twenty years his stature will be even greater than Poe's in the realm which they both made peculiarly their own, no one can really say. But I'm inclined to believe it will be.

Question: Did Lovecraft take occultism very seriously? It has been said that he did—that in his youth he drew magical symbols on the walls and floor of one of the rooms in the Angell Street house, which were found by an elderly physician whose residence it later became.

Answer: That is total nonsense. In all of the many conversations I had with him he never once mentioned such a lapse. And he would have, I'm sure, if he'd passed through even the briefest of a "magical circle" credulity stage. Such an attempt to exorcise the "Powers of Darkness" or summon them to his aid would have seemed to him a silliness meriting nothing but contempt. To have entertained such a thought in a moment of boyish exuberance, if only as a playacting pretense, would have gone just as much against the grain. His disbelief in the occult was absolute.

I'm glad you asked me that question, because I've something quite important to discuss on that very subject, and I've waited much too long to stress its significance in relation to everything I've said…

Question: You mean, he placed no credence whatsoever in the possible reality of cosmic horrors from some timeless *other* world or dimension that might bear at least a slight resemblance to the ones he wrote about?

Answer: Lovecraft was an extreme scientific materialist. He had no patience with anything that went contrary to what modern biochemistry or astrophysics or any other branch of science has revealed about the nature of the universe, or life on this planet. To have allowed himself to hold contrary opinions, even for a moment, while exploring some imaginary Cavern of the Archetypes, would have been unthinkable. It would have undermined too seriously his integrity as a rationalistic thinker.

It's vitally important to keep this in mind at all times. Otherwise you'll have a totally false idea of what he was like. To him the

Cthulhu Mythos was an artistic construct and nothing else. But as an artistic construct it was of supreme importance to him, because he was quite willing to believe that there is something in the dream life of mankind that is magnificent beyond belief, if only because it alone has the power to release us from the tyranny of space and time, and create an illusion of strangeness and mystery and awe that can make life seem meaningful even if, in a cosmic sense, it is wholly without meaning.

I, for one, have always believed that it may well be much more meaningful than Lovecraft was willing to concede. But that is really beside the point. He was a dreamer on the nightside, an explorer of the Great Unknown in a Blakean sense, whether he knew it or not.

We don't know what such a dreamer may discover—we never know. Only the exploration is important, the creation of some tremendous new mythology which, like the Cthulhu Mythos, reveals what the human mind is capable of when it erects no barriers to its exploratory drives. In the Mythos the feeling that Lovecraft enables us to share is that in some wholly indefinable way, there may be other realities beyond that which we know, some ultimate realm of primordial timelessness in which move vast, mysterious shapes antedating by trillions of years the formation of the universe of stars.

Question: Would you say, then, that Lovecraft was a mystic?

Answer: No. Mysticism as it is generally accepted in a traditional sense has come to mean some kind of transcendence associated with various forms of religious belief, whether Far Eastern, Middle Eastern, or Occidental. It is frequently intimately associated with elaborate, ritualistic forms of worship or the taking of drugs. Even when it involves what is referred to today as "Transcendental Meditation" or a lonely withdrawal from external reality to contemplate what St. John of the Cross liked to think brought him into immediate and rapturous communication with God, it excludes from all serious consideration a materialistic approach to reality. Even Blake, who was perhaps more of a mystic in the traditional sense than otherwise, had a side to his nature which was the opposite of mystical. His approach to reality could be so probing and rationalistic that he had much in common with Voltaire and other philosophers of the Age of Reason. His Christian religious mysticism was of a highly unorthodox nature and may well have been four-fifths a mask to cloak the way he actually felt about the universe.

Question: Several people who met and talked with Lovecraft have described his appearance, but with a strange lack of agreement. How would you describe it? He once said he was so far from good looking that it would be very difficult for a woman to "love a face like mine." That may seem an extreme statement, but he has been quoted as making it in a conversation with his future wife, in which Sonia reproached him for lavishing affection on a cat. Did his friends feel that he might have been justified in saying something like that about himself as far as women were concerned, but that apart from the way he may have impressed women there was nothing in the least ugly about his features?

Answer: There certainly wasn't anything in the least ugly about either the shape of his features or his expression. The same thing was said about Lincoln by a few totally undiscerning people who had caught no more than a brief glimpse of him or had been influenced by the caricatures in Civil War period newspapers. But if you could travel back through time and meet Lincoln in person, the "ugly" would, I'm sure, seem the grossest kind of distortion. Lincoln had a rather unusual countenance and so did Lovecraft. Neither of them could have been thought of as routinely good looking. But the poetic sensitivity which Lincoln's features and expression reveal so unmistakably was just as apparent in Lovecraft's features.

There was, it is true, a slight malformation of his jaw, which was noticeable in the region of his lower lip and which does not appear to have existed in photographs taken of him in his boyhood. It may have been largely dental, or due to some slight growth peculiarity such as occurs in a great many people. I never spoke to him about it, and he never mentioned it either conversationally or in any of his letters. But it was of trivial cosmetic significance and may not even have been noticed by strangers meeting him for the first time, unless they were unusually observant.

There is just one other point that requires clarification. In one or two photographs, particularly in one taken by Talman in which we are both standing against a brick wall in Flatbush, he had almost the look of an extreme Blakean visionary, just a little remote from immediate reality. But that kind of expression was very uncharacteristic of HPL and can be explained by the fact, I think, that photographs are occasionally somewhat deceptive, due perhaps to some peculiarity in the gradations of light and shadow when the picture was taken.

And speaking of photographs, it is interesting to note that HPL never carried a camera with him on any of his travels, even though photographs of historical antiquities taken by others delighted him. Photography can be the most expensive of hobbies, and he was keenly aware of that fact.

Question: But it's hard to imagine any hobby which would have given him more pleasure. Was it necessary for him to be quite so cautious in the spending of money? A few photographs taken with a small camera would have cost very little.

Answer: I'm sure he felt that it was necessary if he were to have any money left for the barest of necessities. At one time he cut his food allotment to less than two dollars a week. That would probably be the equivalent of about five dollars today, but it was still appalling.

Question: Didn't he realize that he might be impairing his health by economizing on food to such an extent? Isn't it possible that insufficient food over a long period may have hastened his death?

Answer: I seriously doubt that, although it does not make it less of a tragedy. With his great gifts and his contributions as an artist, Howard should never have been reduced to such an extremity. A well-rounded diet is important, of course—vitamins are important. But he did eat a great deal of cheese, and recent experiments have shown, despite all the claims of vegetarians and health food faddists, that animal protein is man's most valuable single article of diet. Elderly people in failing health have displayed miraculous improvement on a two-thirds protein diet. Alertness, eyesight, muscular coordination improved over a comparatively short period, in an elaborate series of recent laboratory tests.

But I didn't intend to get into a fighting argument over HPL's diet. It is a very touchy subject, I'm sure, with a great many members of this audience. But the legend that HPL starved to death because of poverty is one of those absurdities that I should like to see demolished. The chances of its being true are so remote as to be virtually non-existent, and I've no wish at all to romanticize what remains a different kind of tragedy. To be forced to exercise such extreme economy was a slap at HPL's dignity—both as a man and an artist. He was totally incapable of self-pity, but that does not make it less tragic.

As for his terminal illness—it was diagnosed as intestinal cancer and nephritis. It has never been established that a restricted diet is a direct or indirect cause of cancer. And the combination of cancer and nephritis would have been too coincidental, occurring as they did within a period of months, to make it seem at all likely that the nephritis was not one of the varieties of that disease which can be caused by cancer. There are several different kinds of kidney ailments which were once lumped together under the obsolete term "Bright's Disease" and cancer is often the chief culprit.

Question: It has often been said that Lovecraft eschewed all traditional or legendary horror myths—that vampires, werewolves, and ghouls were conspicuously absent from his stories and that he created something totally new in the genre—entities that were basically science fictional in the sense that they were of cosmic origin, vast and terrifying encroachments on one small planet in a universe so vast that the scope of such encroachments on other planets of other suns, or even beyond the universe of stars, would have given them long practice in conquering and creating stark terror in life forms other than human. Just how valid do you consider this appraisal?

Answer: It is both true and untrue. It has to be greatly qualified. In many of Lovecraft's earlier stories there were distinctly ghoul-like or vampire-like encroachments; *Pickman's Model* is just one of several examples. It is true that even in those stories he took great care to suggest that the monsters were the opposite of traditional in at least one of their aspects—that some hoary, cosmic frightfulness clung to them. They were certainly not ordinary vampires, ghouls, or werewolves. But neither were they lacking in many of the traditional aspects which are associated with man-into-beast transformations and tomb-dwelling horrors in general, particularly ghouls. If Lovecraft had not possessed a wide reading knowledge of the vampire and the large number of equally hideous, closely-related myths in eastern European folklore, they would not have appeared so often in his stories, albeit transformed by his own incomparable macabre imagination.

I'm not speaking here of folklore source material only.

The entire literary tradition in the domain of supernatural horror story writing has made use of this material to such an extent that it would have been impossible for Lovecraft—or Poe or Bierce or any later writer—to have avoided being influenced by the basic concept of a tomb-dwelling entity, with vampirish or ghoulish attributes, wandering about on this side of the grave and preying upon either the living or the recently deceased.

More than most writers in the genre, Lovecraft was *primarily* influenced by the cosmically terrifying, and the later, and much more significant stories mirror that influence. In that respect, in fact, he was far from merely influenced; he created an entire mythology so original that it was peculiar to himself, despite the contributions of other members of the Lovecraft Circle, so that the derivative factor becomes almost negligible.

But he once told me that he had given considerable thought to writing a straight vampire or werewolf story, without departing to any important extent from the traditional mold in which such stories have been cast in the past. He would have been very good at it, and I think it would have given him an unusual kind of pleasure.

In searching about recently for some references to other writers that would enable me to shed a revealing light on some of the more fascinating minor aspects of Lovecraft, I remembered something I'd once read that was perhaps not so minor. Swinburne was capable of parodying himself, but it would be virtually impossible to imagine Poe or Baudelaire doing so. They took themselves far too seriously, with a tragedy-haunted sort of solemnity. But Lovecraft was more like Swinburne in that respect. His mood of the moment could become light, amused, almost jovial in his refusal to take himself with that degree of seriousness. He was not only fully capable of parodying himself; the writing of a straight vampire story would have been a kind of challenge which, at such moments, he would have been capable of accepting with very little hesitation. But the story itself would not have emerged as a parody. His tongue-in-cheek approach would have been quickly forgotten, and such a complete suspension of disbelief miracle would have taken place that one more vampire story classic would have been added to the very few which deserve to be remembered.

Question: The writer to whom Lovecraft has been most often compared is, of course, Poe. How do you feel about the greatness of Poe, as a literary figure? And do you consider Lovecraft the peer of

Poe, as a writer in the same general tradition?

Answer: My own opinion can hardly be of much importance in a matter of such critical moment. It is far more important to compare what has been written about Poe from the middle of the nineteenth century to the present with what has been written about Lovecraft by more than one critic of impressive contemporary stature. My own view may be of some slight interest, however, if only because any writer preoccupied with the sombre or macabre in literature is naturally in a position, regardless of the shortcomings which his own contributions to the genre may exhibit, to be peculiarly sensitive to gradations of excellence in the work of such leading contenders as Poe, Lovecraft, Machen, Bierce, Blackwood, M. R. James, and Walter de la Mare.

I would say that if we consider both Poe and Lovecraft as profoundly original writers—innovators in the best sense of that term—Lovecraft was as great, possibly a little greater than Poe, but only in *one* of two areas in which such originality is of the utmost importance. There are many such areas, and it is not at all unusual for an artist to acquire a legendary significance in three or four of them. But in discussing Poe and Lovecraft, I think we can narrow it down to just two.

Poe was just as much a dreamer on the nightside as Lovecraft. His writings were tomb-shadowed, cypress-haunted, and preoccupied with death as the dark intruder in every carnival procession in which the leaves of some final autumn become a swirling, smothering threat to the merrymakers long before the procession has succumbed to total demoralization. But Poe was also something more. He was a poet of lost loves, and it is a matter of biographical record that more than once in his youth he paid a nighttime visit to the grave of a childhood "Lost Lenore," mourned her passing for hours, and did not arise before dawn.

Now such behavior may be considered aberrational—the wildest, most extravagant kind of romanticism—and in a sense, it was. But it must also be remembered that Poe was a lyrical poet of major stature, who made that intensity of emotion, that abandonment to an imperishable sort of human grief and despair, an American legend as authentic as *Moby Dick,* or Whitman's vision of future democratic vistas in a new and different America, or Emily Dickinson's lonely vigil as a solitary dreamer at odds with the world.

In that respect, I've always felt that Poe was greater than Lovecraft. But in the realm which they both made peculiarly their own—that of supernatural horror and terror on a cosmic plane (and there was much of the cosmic in the most powerful of Poe's stories)—Lovecraft was perhaps preeminent.

Question: But Lovecraft was *also* a poet. What you're really saying is that he wasn't nearly as great a poet. Or am I mistaken?

Answer: It is certainly true that he was not a lyrical poet remotely comparable to Poe. But that is not what I'm really saying. Lovecraft was simply incapable of becoming torn apart by an imperishable, eternity-defying romantic attachment. A mad love would have seemed to him absurd, and not the slightest impulse in that direction could have arisen in him. He was simply incapable of experiencing intense passion on that level. He was capable of deep affection, and I'm quite sure that if his wife had died in the early days of their marriage it would have been a great blow to him. He would have grieved, quite deeply. He was the opposite, as I've said many times, of cold and unemotional. But a mad love, no.

He was even spared both the glory and the tragic aspects of a hopeless infatuation in which such love is not returned. To have never experienced such an infatuation is to have missed something very wonderful, despite its scar-inflicting potential. But Lovecraft bore no such scars. Life wounded him in other ways, but never in that way.

Question: But just how does all of that make Poe a greater literary figure?

Answer: I knew that question was coming. It can be answered quite simply. Poe, in both his life and his writings, added something on a literary level to the innermost fabric of human experience that would otherwise have been missing. The *idealization* of a mad love carried to its utmost extreme of intensity. A mad love or a lost love—they are very much the same. It has been carried to almost as great an extreme by other writers, but in Poe, even more than in Keats, it became an imperishable obsession, heightened by the irreversible tragedy of eternal separation in time and space, or a reunion that could not be other than illusionary in "a tomb by the sounding sea."

Question: But isn't it a little unfair to add that side of Poe to your comparison? After all—

Answer: I'm being unfair with a purpose, to try to demonstrate that it is always a mistake to draw too close a parallel between two writers who have much in common. Poe was Poe and Lovecraft was Lovecraft. Why not let it rest that way? If Lovecraft was not quite the literary immortal that Poe has been to generations of readers, he will still have a permanent place in American literature. In his own right, Lovecraft was one of the few writers who possessed a vision that set him a little apart and made him unique in his generation and, I'm convinced, in many generations to come.

Only Baudelaire was comparable to Poe as a tragic "dreamer of dreams, wandering by lone sea breakers and sitting by desolate streams," a dreamer so haunted by visions of love and death that no other human condition, even that of the poverty which they both shared, could have seemed quite so all-obsessive. But Lovecraft was *also* a writer of genius, and almost as lonely in many ways; and poverty dogged his footsteps just as persistently. What Baudelaire said of Poe, and by implication about himself—"Some men are born with the word 'Luckless' engraven on their foreheads in letters of fire"— could also have been said of Lovecraft.

And in view of his tomb-shadowed, macabre visions, and his darkly enduring, cosmic Cthulhu Mythos, the qualities which go into the creation of a literary legend are present in him as abundantly as any romantically-disposed biographer could desire. And there will always be such biographers as well as scalpel-equipped, totally realistic ones to do full justice to his extraordinary aspects both as a writer and as a man. And this is as it should be. I have no quarrel with either school, since I've always felt they are opposite faces of the same coin, and both are essential to take full measure of an artist. In Lovecraft's case, that measure will, I think, grow larger and more worthy of respect, and even awe, with every passing year.

Question: But Poe is not as widely read today as he was when Lovecraft placed him on so high a pedestal. And he may not be in the future, even if there is a brief Poe revival. Might that not be just as true of Lovecraft?

Answer: Of course. Every important American writer has passed through periods of great critical acclaim and near-eclipse. Melville was almost forgotten—he never, in fact, was considered a writer of great importance in his lifetime—but there was a great Melville revival in the 1920s, and although it may have leveled a bit in recent years, his fame is now secure. There have been several periods when Poe was generally considered far less significant an author than Emerson, Thoreau, or Whitman. But what is most interesting is the fact that like Lovecraft, he *is* being widely read today. More widely, in fact, than he was forty years ago, especially among the young. Not only is interest in Lovecraft sweeping American college campuses on an unprecedented scale; it is paralleled by a Poe revival. Professor Herbert Edwards of the New York University English Department has called Poe an amazingly durable figure, and I firmly believe that fifty years from now Lovecraft will rival him in durability.

Question: Everyone who knew Lovecraft quite well seems to have been convinced that there was something that set him apart, not only from the average run of individuals, but from a great many quite exceptional individuals. Could you elaborate on that a little more?

Answer: It was basically, I think, just one quality, but it has two important aspects. One of them can be best exemplified by dwelling for a moment on his total refusal to consider the monetary factor when some young author wrote to him for the first time and enclosed a story or poem, accompanied by a request for advice or criticism. Never once would it have occurred to him to regard the writer as a possible future client. Revision and ghost-writing comprised the main source of his income, but his letters of advice were written for one reason only—there was in him so deeply experienced an understanding of what it meant to be a beginning writer of talent who was still uncertain as to how that talent should be developed and channeled, that a total kindliness took over and he spent long hours in correspondence that afforded him not the slightest financial remuneration.

Another aspect of the difference I shall try to make as comprehensible as possible, although it involves certain rather elusive intangibles. He had a total lack of the driving egotism that is inseparable from self-seeking aggressiveness. He was not lacking in aggressiveness when there was some small, but grievous wrong or some great injustice to be challenged and eliminated, but he was far more a creative than an aggressive personality. There is a great difference here, and I've always felt that before "extreme aggressiveness" you almost always can place the adjective "sadistic."

It may well be that a new kind of man is coming into existence, as so many fiction writers have predicted, and that Howard may have been one of the few forerunners. The English actor, Trevor Howard, once said that whenever he encountered extreme aggressiveness in anyone, man or woman, he put as much distance as possible between that individual and himself.

CHAPTER NINETEEN

In just the past two years at least four biographers have embarked upon a daring new approach to biography, seemingly designed to give the reader as much of a jolt as an X-rated movie would have done if it could have been administered as shock therapy to an elderly New England spinster of five generations ago. This new, startlingly innovative departure adopts as its guiding principle what in the X-rated vernacular might be summed up by the phrase "letting it all hang out." Unhappily for those who have been misled into favoring such a departure, there are a great many people—and HPL was one of them—who have no dark, hidden motivations or secrets that could be successfully exploited in this way.

The only aspect of HPL's complex personality that has caused some consternation among those who never met him and who thus have only a hazy notion of what he was really like, has long since ceased to be a secret; for three volumes of his correspondence are now in print and in all three there appear several letters that make how he felt about the superiority of the Anglo-Saxon culture stream, both in Europe and America, unmistakably explicit. Such were his feelings at one time and not in his later years, but I shall clarify that presently. What is most important to stress at this point is the degree of light I am in a position to shed upon this from the many conversations I had with him when we were discussing other matters. During all of those talks on long walks through the streets of New York and Providence, I never once heard him utter a derogatory remark about any member of a minority group who passed him on the street or had occasion to engage him in conversation, whose cultural or racial antecedents differed from his own.

There can be no denial that the letters I have mentioned contain passages which today would be considered racially prejudiced, or that in one of his stories, *The Horror at Red-Hook,* and in his conversations with me, he did refer to "a vast alien horde" with which he professed to have nothing in common. But a generalized kind of emotionally held racial or cultural prejudice is quite a different thing from the application of such a prejudice on a personal level. The two may overlap to a slight extent, of course; they could hardly fail to do so. But in Howard they were very different in many important ways.

Dr. Dirk W. Mosig, Assistant Professor of Psychology at Georgia Southwestern College, has come eloquently to HPL's defense in that area, and he has graciously given me permission to quote at length from one of his recent letters. It is so completely in accord with my own views that I can think of no better way of treating this matter than to present it here in its entirety, accompanied by a few personal comments which attest to the validity of what Professor Mosig has said:

> The often heard allegation that H. P. Lovecraft was a "racist" is not only false, but highly misleading. Portions of his letters—primarily written for his aunts and not intended for publication—are taken out of the context provided by Lovecraft's milieu, his life style, and the temper of the times, and misconstrued to imply that H. P. Lovecraft was a Hitlerian monster dreaming of exterminating racial minorities. Nothing could be further from the truth.
>
> First of all the word "racist" carries today connotations quite different from the meaning the term had in the first third of the century. During that period the superiority of the Caucasian culture was accepted matter-of-factly by the overwhelming majority of HPL's contemporaries. This concept was not really challenged in a significant manner until the atrocities of World War II produced a major change in public opinion. While today, in the postwar era, it is conceivable that a person expressing HPL's views could be called a "racist," it is certainly completely unfair to apply modern standards to judge the private statements of a gentleman who died years before the last global conflagration.
>
> In the second place, Lovecraft, like anyone else, deserves to be judged by his behavior, rather than by private statements made with no intention to injure another. All those who knew HPL confirm that he was always kind and considerate to others, regardless of their ethnical or social backgrounds. A true gentleman, he abstained from behavior—verbal or motor—likely to hurt anyone. The accusation of anti-Semitism is particularly ludicrous in the case of HPL, some of whose best friends, and even his very wife, were Jewish. When did he discriminate, when did he attack, verbally or physically, a member of any minority group? HPL certain-

ly did not behave like a racist in any manner, and it is the behavior that counts.

In the third place, as Dr. Brobst (Dr. Harry K. Brobst, Professor of Psychology, Oklahoma State University) has pointed out, HPL presented different poses or "personas" to his various correspondents and friends. This was part of his unique charm, his ability to adapt himself congenially to the personalities of others. To E. Hoffmann Price, for instance, he appeared as a playful extrovert, while to others he sounded like an introverted philosopher, and yet to others he was a youthful pal, or wise old Grandpa Theobald. It is likely that he also appeared to his aunts as they wished him to be, that some of his "racist" statements were made, not out of deep conviction, but out of a desire to be congenial with the views held by others. This does not indicate a weakness of character, but instead points toward an understanding nature tolerant of the views of others.

HPL did not hate blacks, Jews, Italians, or any other minorities. But as a lover of the eighteenth century and New England architecture and traditions, he resented the destruction of the sites and cultural landmarks of the past by immigrants and others to whom he felt these meant little. While respecting the value of other cultures, he desired to preserve New England culture from the onslaught of alien traditions and ways of life. He was a traditionalist, a lover of the past, not a rabid racist in any sense. And in his later years, even this resentment toward alien cultures waned, and he entertained extremely liberal views coupled with his lifelong tolerance and understanding of others.

To label H. P. Lovecraft a "racist" is absurd and ludicrous, and reflects at best a total lack of understanding of the life of the admirable gentleman from Providence.

Just the fact, of course, that a man's friends are Jewish or Italian or Scandinavian is not in itself significant. But when such friends, knowing the worst, remain steadfast in their loyalty for forty years, with no diminishment in their affection and esteem, it means a great deal.

My wife is Jewish, and though she never met HPL, her testimony when she read the letters recently for the first time should, I feel, be made part of this record, because it helps to make more readily understandable how those friends felt about HPL at the time and still feel today.

"A few of the passages sound terrible, I know," she told me. "But I don't think he was in the least like the way they sound—not really, not deep down. Far too much kindliness shines through the pages of his correspondence, considered as a whole. It seems like the kind of distortion that he couldn't help, that was partly forced on him by the views his family held and partly by his fear, particularly in his New York days, that his anchorage to a certain, long-established tradition which linked him to a past in which he felt more secure was in some way being jeopardized. His lack of the wealth which so many members of old families seem to feel they need to maintain such a tradition unimpaired in their personal lives may have made that fear, unconscious to a great extent, more irrational in its manifestations than it might otherwise have been. I don't think he ever felt that his heritage made him a superior individual. It was just—something very precious to him that he felt was being threatened by different culture streams that seemed alien to him."

"There wasn't the slightest trace of snobbishness in his nature," I assured her. "If there had been, I would have known. There is nothing quite as difficult to conceal, for Freudian slips aren't even needed to bring it to the attention of a child of four in a five minute conversation."

During the last few years of his life Howard repudiated the views he had held until about the age of forty or forty-one. And he was so appalled and sickened by an account of what was taking place in Berlin in 1936 by a Providence schoolteacher acquaintance who had just returned from a visit to Germany that he drew a portrait of Hitler in one of his last letters to me that would have made Pickman's model, by comparison, seem an almost benign kind of monster.

CHAPTER TWENTY

Three months before HPL's last, fatal illness—a combination of nephritis and intestinal cancer—he wrote me that he was looking forward to another New York visit. "Looking forward" was not the way he would have phrased it had he been in the slightest doubt concerning his ability to make the trip, since he planned such excursions carefully in advance and would never have committed himself to that extent if he had felt his plans might go awry. But usually when such trips were in prospect he kept in frequent touch with me by letter, knowing that I would have to arrange lodging for him with a family who lived on the third floor of our apartment building.

When several weeks went by and I did not hear from him again, I became puzzled. Then I received a postcard saying that he had had several quite severe attacks of indigestion and his physician had advised him to have some clinical tests made at a Providence hospital. He shared my dislike of hospitals and made it plain that the prospect did not make him at all happy. "But I imagine I can stand it for two or three days," he wrote. "I'm still looking forward to that visit."

I responded immediately, asking him to keep me informed on the results of the tests. But a considerable period went by before I received another postcard. And it was not from Howard. It was a special delivery message from James F. Morton, informing me that Howard was critically ill and that it had all been so sudden that his aunt had been unable to leave the hospital long enough to put a phone call through to anyone; the news had come to him indirectly through a Providence friend who knew Mrs. Gamwell.

I tried to contact the hospital by phone but had no success and was on my way to a Western Union office when I picked up a morning newspaper, as one will sometimes do to distract one's thoughts for a moment from news that does not bear thinking about. It was the *New York Times*.

And there it was, in not more than fifteen lines of type—far down, I believe, on one of the inner pages. I only remember with certainty the type seemed darker than the surrounding columns—far darker and heavier. "WRITER CHARTS FATAL MALADY" And then the terrible finality of it rushed upon me.

At such moments it is not an old friend's achievements one remembers most, no matter how great. It is all the times one has met and talked with him, the visits planned in advance, and the unexpected ones, the joyful, sad, funny, terribly human incidents which have accompanied such meetings across the years.

I saw HPL again on Cape Cod, where he had joined me on a summer vacation trip to Provincetown and back. I saw him wading out to a ramshackle, barnstorming type hydroplane, to which I never would have entrusted myself, and disappearing from view on his first and only airplane ride—a ten minute, harbor-encircling journey at the bargain price of two dollars.

Then my vision shifted to a centuries-old cemetery in Flatbush, as HPL was stooping to pick up a small, square fragment of a disintegrating tombstone that had fallen to the ground, and carrying it home with him. I saw him placing it on the mantel in his book-lined living room, between an imitation Wedgewood vase and a dried, crusted object which he had picked up on a New England beach. It could have been a sun-blackened piece of driftwood, but it bore a disturbing resemblance to a monkey's paw.

I saw him at the famous marine biological station at Woods Hole, Massachusetts, walking along a stone pier that extended far out into the bay, then standing at the end of the pier staring down, as if the green water that swirled and eddied about the piles below might have been set into motion by some hidden horror from the depths that would rise terrifyingly into view if he waited long enough.

A moment later he was retracing his steps and signing the enormous ledger where a record was kept of all visitors to the station. And I could hear myself again making a prankish suggestion that seems just a little unforgivable in retrospect. "Just to give the next visitor an unexpected start"—I am not certain those were my exact words—"sign it *Edgar Allan Poe*. Why not? The marine biologists who drift in and out here have a superlative sense of humor—exceptionally gifted research scientists usually do. It will astound them and set them chuckling. And visitors could still be wondering about that signature a century from now."

"Well, why not indeed," I can recall him saying. He signed the guest book simply *Edgar Poe,* exactly as Poe had often done. And I am prepared to take a solemn oath that the calligraphy, with a curved line beneath it, bore a much closer resemblance to that of the writer from Baltimore than it did to the more flowing signature of HPL.

Of course I could not sign my own name after that, for it would have suggested that Poe had visited the station in the company of a nonentity. In what I am utterly certain could not have been more than a close approximation of my exact words, I told him, "Just for the hell of it I'm going to add to the mystery," and put down *Algernon Charles Swinburne.*

If any dedicated Lovecraftian scholar is curious about this and cares to visit the Woods Hole station today, I know he will find those signatures still there, for guest books of that nature are usually preserved for a considerable number of years, even though that particular volume may have to be taken down from a high shelf and may well have become stippled, cover to cover, with the riddlings of shipworms.

EPILOGUE: LOVECRAFT AND POE

Poe probably influenced Lovecraft more than any other writer in a significant, direction-pointing manner. So great was his admiration for the Baltimore dreamer that one clear, bright October day over half a century ago, Howard and I set out, in the company of James F. Morton, on a journey to the Fordham shrine.

The Poe cottage has remained unchanged for a great many more autumns than the ones that Poe immortalized in verse, for he saw the leaves turn sere not more than forty times in his life. Probably thirty-five times would be a more accurate figure, for a few of the years "too wild for song" were spent in the deep South.

We were accompanied also by a young college student no older than myself, whose name I have forgotten—understandable, perhaps, since I met him only once, but unforgivable in view of the fact that he was armed with a Brownie camera and was kind enough to mail me a photograph the following week which I cherish to this day. Someone had to take the picture, and he does not appear in it even as a shadow, which meant, of course, that only Morton and the present writer will enjoy the kind of immortality which anyone portrayed as standing at HPL's side in front of that particular cottage seems certain to possess as long as Poe and Lovecraft remain bracketed in the same general frame of reference in the years to come.

Prophetic as that photograph has proved itself to be, it was no more astonishing than the words which Morton spoke a few minutes after the picture was taken, and before we entered the cottage.

Standing on the lawn in the bright October sunlight a few feet from the cottage, Howard had murmured: "The past, the past! How everything here makes the years seem to fall away. There will never be another Poe." Then he removed from his coatpocket one of his quite early stories, *Hypnos,* and dedicated it to Poe, letting the wind rumple the pages a little, I think deliberately, as if hoping it would be carried from his hand into the cottage and come to rest beside the carved wooden raven just inside one of the small-paned windows.

What Morton said was very much to the point. "Such extreme reverence is hardly justified, in a writer who will someday be recognized as Poe's peer."

Why could not I have said something of that sort? No one could have admired more the story which Howard was holding in his hand. Unhappily my critical judgment, immature as it was at the time, still made me unable to believe that Morton had not gone out on a limb.

After all, Poe had been Poe.

www.ingramcontent.com/pod-product-compliance
Lightning Source LLC
LaVergne TN
LVHW041624070426
835507LV00008B/432